BACK TO BASIC™

ACTING IN LEADERSHIP

Scott M. Carter

Scott M. Carter Publishing

Forest Lake, Minnesota

Scott M. Carter/Scott M. Carter Publishing

Forest Lake, MN 55025

www.scottmcarter.com (publishing permissions)

Book Layout ©2017 BookDesignTemplates.com

Cover Design https://selfpubbookcovers.com/Narateen

Back to BASIC™: Acting In Leadership/ Scott M. Carter. —1st ed.

ISBN 979-8-9879170-2-2

Permissions:

Back To BASIC™ book series

There Is No Such Thing As Business Leadership

Back To BASIC™: Acting In Leadership

The Bible Teaches Acting In Leadership

Back To BASIC™: Let's Do Business

Leadership: Achieving Optimal Effectiveness

Thank you to my incredible wife Lisa, my family, and my friends who support my efforts to continue writing with a focus on serving others. Thank you to everyone who inspires me to act in leadership and thank you to my readers who support my works.

Acting in leadership is what makes a person a leader.
~Scott M. Carter.

Disclaimer:

The material in this book is not a substitute for professional advice, psychotherapy, diagnosis, treatment, psychological care, or professional medical treatment and care. Content is for educational purposes only.

This publication contains the opinions of its author and is intended to provide helpful and informative material on the subjects addressed. The author and publisher are not engaged in rendering medical, health, or any other kind of professional services. The reader should consult his or her medical, health, or other competent professional before adopting any of the suggestions in this book.

The author and publisher specifically disclaim all responsibility for any liability, loss, or risk, personal or otherwise, which is incurred as a consequence, directly or indirectly, of the use and application of any of the contents of this book.

Contents

Preface

"There is no such thing as business leadership," is a bold statement. I make that argument in my second book, *There Is No Such Thing As Business Leadership*. All of the 800-plus definitions of leadership that exist today were born out of misguidedly attaching leadership to a position in a hierarchy and associating leadership with doing business.

If the above claims are valid, I must back them up with proof of what constitutes leadership in its true essence. The Back to BASIC Leadership blueprint defines when a person is acting in leadership.

This book, *Back to BASIC™: Acting in Leadership*, delves into the history and sources that contain the attributes and actions of leadership. When you finish this book, you will have the knowledge to confidently determine when you are acting in leadership and, thus, a leader.

Introduction

A knight's Tale

The film *A Knight's Tale* hit the movie theaters in 2001. The story setting portrays life in the 1300s. Three of the Characters, William Thatcher, played by Heath Ledger, Roland, played by Mark Addy, and Wat, played by Alan Tudyk, are all peasant squires. Peasant squires served noble lords and knights. Nobility in the fourteenth century implied a person was of royalty based on their family lineage. Peasants were considered lower class and could not be noble. The movie is fiction, but the premise of nobility isn't fiction; it was a reality of those times.

You see, to be noble in the fourteenth century meant you belonged to a hereditary class with high social or political status. Nobility was a position in society, not how a person behaved.

In this movie, the noble Lord that William, Roland, and Wat served died. They decided to pretend that William was of nobility. They did this so they could compete in jousting tournaments to earn money to eat and survive.

During their journey, the three characters encountered a naked man walking along a dirt road. That character's name? Geoffrey Chaucer. It turns out that Chaucer was a real person.

Geoffrey Chaucer was an English poet, author, and civil servant best known for *The Canterbury Tales*. He has been called "the father of English literature" and "the father of English poetry." He was the first writer to be buried in what has since come to be called Poets' Corner in Westminster Abbey. Chaucer's birthdate is unknown, but his death occurred on October 25, 1400, in London.

In the movie *A Knight's Tale*, Paul Bettany plays Chaucer, a poet and writer who is also a gambler and a liar. That is no coincidence. Authors of books and writers of movie scripts often attach the names of historical figures to the characters in their books or movies.

The tales written by the real Chaucer teach us life lessons. The writers of the movie *A Knight's Tale* portray the character of Chaucer as a liar and a gambler seeking a quick fortune. The writers did so not because this was how the real Chaucer lived but because the real Chaucer wrote stories to teach us about those undesirable attributes. Many movies are written intentionally to teach us lessons about acting in leadership. We need to open our eyes to see this.

The Canterbury Tales

The Canterbury Tales, written by the real Chaucer, includes the story of three men who wanted revenge on death. They set out to find Death and kill him because Death took their friend from them.

As they set out on this journey, they came upon an elderly man walking along the same dirt road where they traveled. The men inquired if this stranger knew where they might find Death. The man told them they could locate him at the foot of an oak tree and then pointed them in the direction of the mighty oak.

When the three men arrive at the tree, they find a large hoard of gold coins. The magnificence of this treasure causes them to forget about their quest to kill Death.

The shiny, sparkling riches hypnotize the men, and greed overcomes them. One of the three men advises the other two that it is best to wait until dark to bring the gold back to town. This plan will help to keep their new treasure a secret. The other two men agree.

While they wait for darkness to set in, one man suggests that one of them should go to town and get some wine and bread to feast on.

One man volunteers to go to town for bread and wine. After his departure, the two remaining men plot to kill him upon his return, thus increasing their share of the gold. The plot thickens [suspenseful music plays, ♫ *dun dun duuuuunnnnnn* ♫].

The man who volunteered to go to town had the same thought of keeping the gold all to himself. He purchased some wine and put poison in two of the bottles with the intent of having the other two men drink that wine.

While they conceive these treacherous plans, it does not occur to them that the others might have the same idea. Therefore, each party does not know of the other's evil ambitions. When the man who went to town for bread and wine returns, the two men kill him. They then celebrate by drinking the wine, dying slow and painful deaths. Would you, the reader, be able to tell us the lessons gained from this story?

Revenge can bring us face-to-face with Death. Greed can kill a person before their time is up, and no one can cheat Death.

The elderly man they encountered on the road was Death himself. Seeking revenge brought them face-to-face with death. Death then used greed to get the men to kill each other. Death did not kill them; they killed each other. One might assume this is quite a unique plot for something written in the 1300s. It is not. Chaucer is a great writer, but these life lessons have existed for much longer.

The bad news? These lessons seem to be going unnoticed or purposefully ignored. The magnificent news is that these lessons *exist,* and they continue to be carried forward into current-day books and movies, where, if we so choose, we can use them to teach lessons of acting in leadership.

Harry Potter and the Deathly Hallows

J.K. Rowling, the author of the Harry Potter series of books, participated in a July 2007 webchat hosted by her publisher, Bloomsbury. Rowling shared how "The Pardoner's Tale" of Geoffrey Chaucer's *Canterbury Tales* inspired her folktale used in *Harry Potter and the Deathly Hallows,* Part One. She named it "The Tale of the Three Brothers." It is an incredible story, based on Chaucer's equally seductive tale, with multiple lessons built into it. As they say in England, "Not good. Brilliant!"

Anyone who has read the Harry Potter series of books or watched the movies knows that wizards, witches, and magic set the stage for the world in which Harry Potter exists.

In Rowling's story, "The Tale of the Three Brothers," the brothers use magic to make a bridge over a dangerous river. By doing so, they potentially cheat death by avoiding the deep, menacing waters. Muggles, the name for nonmagical people, would need to cross the river without using magic, giving death its shot at taking their lives.

Displeased with the three brothers' use of magic to evade him, Death appears on the bridge as they attempt to cross. He cunningly feigns admiration for their cleverness and offers them rewards of their choosing. This twist, reminiscent of "The Pardoner's Tale" by

Geoffrey Chaucer, adds a layer of complexity to Rowling's narrative. It is a testament to the rich tapestry of literary influences that shape her storytelling.

The first brother chooses something that would make him the most powerful wizard in the world—seeking ultimate power leads quickly to his death. The second brother chooses something that would allow him to cheat death, to bring a person back to life once they die. No one can cheat death; it is inevitable, and in his attempt to cheat death, he ended up taking his own life.

And the third brother? He was suspicious of being rewarded for something that did not merit such acknowledgment. To him, building a bridge using magic was not a great deed. He knew that creating the bridge was a misuse of the gift of magic, the position of power they, the three brothers, possessed.

When it is the third brother's turn to receive his undeserved reward, he chooses something that allows him to go quietly on with his life unnoticed. To seek power, riches, or fame would put him in death's crosshairs. He lived his life humbly, gratefully, and with integrity, raising his son. After raising his son, he then passed the gift he received from death onto his son so his son could live the same way. He then willingly gave himself to death.

The additional lesson in Rowling's story is that no matter what one has done in the past, *the decision you make now is what matters.* When one decides to be humble, live with humility, act with integrity, and be full of gratitude, a person can live a long, purposeful life that can provide rewards beyond that of power or material possessions. He had a son, and he could watch his son grow into a man who carried the traits of humility, humbleness, gratefulness, and integrity into the future.

Back to BASIC™: Acting in Leadership

This book, the one you are reading right now, is about acting in leadership. The lessons about acting in leadership are all around us. They existed back when old Sanskrit was written, through the writings of Plato and Socrates, of Lao Tzu and Buddha, within the writings of the *Bible*, and yes, in most of the modern books and movies we all love. The lessons for "acting in leadership" existed long before the current definitions of leadership were invented.

In the wizarding world, Rowling created a fictitious author, Beedle the Bard, who wrote *The Tale of the Three Brothers*. The message that Rowling passes onto us, the readers, is that parents in the wizarding world could use this wizarding world children's book to teach life lessons to their kids.

Through the stories within, the book teaches where the misuse of magic will lead them. It teaches a person not to seek power and, when you are in a position of authority, not to misuse that position. It appears that we have lost the art of teaching leadership lessons, in their true essence, in the real world.

If you have read my first two books, then you know that much of this lost art of acting in leadership is because we ended up attaching leadership to a position in a hierarchy and also associating it with doing business. If you have not read either of those books, that's ok. You will not need that information to get everything you need from this book. If you have read them, then parts of this book will seem like an old friend showing up with a warm plate of cookies and an infectious smile.

CHAPTER ONE

BASIC™ Leadership Blueprint

Stories containing lessons on how to act in leadership have existed for thousands of years. The lessons are not new, and they have not changed in their true essence. We began to change them, shifting what it means to act in leadership. This transformation occurred during the industrialization of the United States and the world.

Suppose we went back and visited the early writings of philosophers, storytelling through parables, fables, and moral lessons of the last twenty-five hundred years. Would we find a series of common threads that could help us define when a person acts in leadership? The answer is *yes!*

Seven components help us define when a person acts in leadership—Belief, Action, Success, Insight, Collaboration, Integrity, and the Leadership Lifeline.

The BASIC™ Leadership Outer Ring

Success is neither magical nor mysterious. Success is the natural consequence of consistently applying basic fundamentals. ~Jim Rohn

The acronym BASIC stands for Belief, Action, Success, Insight, and Collaboration. BASIC leadership illustrates the fundamentals of life and the first part of acting in leadership. Below is the definition of each of the first five components depicted in the image on the next page.

> - Belief—Trust, Faith, or Confidence in Someone or Something.
> - Action—To Take Action; Do Something
> - Success—The Result from Taking Action Toward a Worthy Ideal
> - Insight—The Capacity to Gain an Accurate and Intuitive Understanding
> - Collaboration—Joining with Someone or Something to Produce or Create

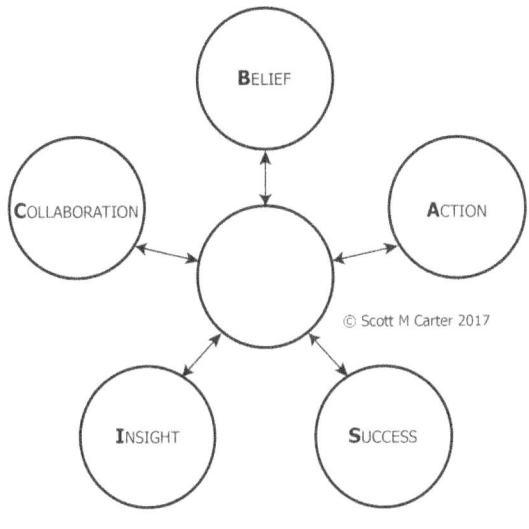

Back to BASIC™
Leadership Outer Ring

Let's begin with the first component that makes up the outer ring of what I have coined as the BASIC™ Leadership blueprint.

Beliefs

If you were asked what drives your actions every day, how would you respond? That question can be answered with a single word. Beliefs.

Believing in something will not make it true. However, people will or will not act based on what they believe. Believing defines and creates our lives. We see it everywhere in modern times, back to the early philosophers thousands of years ago.

Walt Disney knew this and helped us to act on it. *The Wonderful World of Disney* first aired on October 27, 1954. In 1961, it moved to NBC so people could see it in color. "The following program is brought to you in living color," the voice on our TV would proclaim. Children across the nation would smile and wriggle with anticipation as they viewed the fairytale castle engulfed in fireworks while the magical Disney tune played. That same image and music are still used today at the beginning of all the remarkable stories that Disney created. Walt tells us to use our imagination. He encourages us all to begin by believing.

> *When you believe in a thing, believe in it all the way, implicitly and unquestionably.* ~Walt Disney

In 1937 Napoleon Hill published his book *Think and Grow Rich*. The primary premise of his book? Our beliefs. When we being with our beliefs, money, fame, power, contentment, peace of mind, and happiness are ours. Hill uses the term "think" because rational thought is also part of his teachings, but we must start by believing first. Read his book, and you'll find that beliefs are the underlying driver for a person's actions.

> *I believe in being strong when everything seems to be going wrong. I believe that happy girls are the prettiest girls. I believe that tomorrow is another day, and I believe in miracles.* ~Audry Hepburn

The future belongs to those who believe in the beauty of their dreams. ~Eleanor Roosevelt

Many of the strongest women role models enlightened us about the power of our beliefs.

To believe in something and not to live it is dishonest. ~Mahatma Gandhi

Mohandas Karamchand Gandhi was an Indian lawyer, anti-colonial nationalist, and political ethicist who employed nonviolent resistance to lead the successful campaign for India's independence from British rule. He inspired movements for civil rights and freedom across the world. His belief in civil rights led to his actions, driving toward a worthy ideal. Martin Luther King Jr. had many of the same worthy ideals as Gandhi.

I believe that unarmed truth and unconditional love will have the final word in reality. This is why right, temporarily defeated, is stronger than evil triumphant. ~Martin Luther King Jr.

Pick any culture, ethnicity, or gender, and you'll find quotes about the power of our beliefs. Make a list of your favorite movies and look for that moment when some character addresses beliefs. One of my favorites is from the Star Wars Series.

The film *The Empire Strikes Back* was released in 1980. The main character, Luke Skywalker, a soon-to-be Jedi Knight, is training with an 800-year-old Jedi Master named Yoda. In one scene, Luke attempts to raise a fighter jet out of a swamp using the force. He fails. Then

Yoda lifts his arm, closes his eyes, raises the fighter jet out of the swamp, and sets it onto solid ground.

Watching in amazement, Luke turns to Yoda and says, "I don't believe it." And Yoda responds, "That is why you fail."

Does this mean we will begin to lift spaceships out of swamps because the subject of beliefs now has scientific evidence for being an extremely powerful influence on our habits, choices, and happiness? No, do not be silly. However, we absolutely know through physics and science that our beliefs play a massive role in our behaviors. Many people will not even try acting in leadership because they believe they will fail based on false assumptions.

I love how movie writers toss in language that tells us things before something is revealed later in the movie. Luke's father, Anakin Skywalker, turns to the dark side and takes the name Darth Vader. In German, Vader means father. His new name is literally Darth Father. A person watching this in Germany would hear the emperor say, "You will now be known as Darth Father." It is not quite as menacing sounding.

Later in the series, the conversation could have gone like this: "Luke, I am your father." Luke responds, "No, I don't believe it." Darth Vader replies, "Uh, no, really. My name is Darth Father. Think about it."

In his book, *As a Man Thinketh* (1903), James Allen addresses our beliefs. People often quote this book regarding beliefs. Again, when Allen or others use the word "think," they are talking about what we "believe."

A man is literally what he thinks, his character being the complete sum of all his thoughts. ~James Allen

Radio was in its infancy around 1905 and grew dramatically through 1925. When it comes to radio and beliefs, we find a significant event that occurred in the 1950s.

Earl Nightingale was an American radio speaker and author dealing with the subjects of human character development, motivation, and meaningful existence. At this time, radio had begun to play a vital role in getting information to the masses.

In 1957, Nightingale hosted a live broadcast he named The Strangest Secret. He explained the power of our beliefs in a manner so simple that anyone could understand it. By December 2019, his 31-minute audio broadcast had upwards of 5 million views on YouTube between the multiple postings. Here is one of Nightingale's many quotes.

Whatever we plant in our subconscious mind and nourish with repetition and emotion will one day become a reality. To achieve success, you need to think success. Your thoughts should reflect a positive attitude toward life, and they should affirm the belief that you will be successful. ~Earl Nightingale

Have you ever heard of the Book *As A Man Thinketh* by James Allen or *The Strangest Secret* by Earl Nightingale? Probably not.

François-Marie Arouet is the birth name of Voltaire. Born in 1684 in France, Voltaire believed, above all, in the efficacy of reason. He believed social progress could be achieved through reason and that no authority—religious, political, or otherwise—should be immune to challenge by reason. In his work, Voltaire emphasized the importance of tolerance, especially religious tolerance.

Not only did he have beliefs of his own, as we all do, but he also provided lessons about the power of beliefs.

> *Those who can make you believe absurdities can make you commit atrocities.* ~Voltaire

Pick a time and society, and you'll find philosophical debates containing the same underlying components about people's beliefs and actions. I could go on with hundreds of references.

Understanding the concept of beliefs is easy. I can say, "I believe there is more out there, so I continue to search. Or I do not believe there is more out there, so I do not search." Beliefs drive both action and inaction. For humans, any action taken or not taken is based on some belief. That brings us to our second component of the BASIC Leadership platform, Action.

CHAPTER TWO

From Beliefs To Action

Action

Knowledge without action is wastefulness, and action without knowledge is foolish. ~Al-Ghazâlî

Abu Hamid Muhammad ibn al-Ghazâlî was one of Sunni Islam's most prominent and influential philosophers, theologians, jurists, and mystics around 1058 to 1111 AD. He is considered to be, after the prophet Muhammad, the foremost authority on Islamic theology and jurisprudence.

A person's incentive to take any action is driven by whether they believe it can happen. Action encompasses synonyms such as initiative, work, effort, achievement, and endeavor.

Action is the foundational key to all success. ~Pablo Picasso

Action speaks louder than words, but not nearly as often. ~Mark Twain

Inaction

Action is a great restorer and builder of confidence. Inaction is not only the result, but the cause, of fear. Perhaps the action you take will be successful; perhaps different action or adjustments will have to follow. But any action is better than no action at all. ~Norman Vincent Peale

As Norman Peale states, inaction is also an action and the cause of fear. As we will soon learn, it is also a cause of stress and anxiety, both detrimental to our health.

If you plan to present the argument of, "Well, I didn't act; Therefore, the action component doesn't hold water," that would be a misguided belief. Not taking action is still taking action. It is the same as someone putting two choices in front of you, and you decide not to choose either; you have still made a choice. The third choice is the action of not making a choice. Most people need to learn this simple principle. Not taking action is still taking action. That action is to do nothing. We are always taking some sort of action, even if that action is to do nothing.

The Canadian Rock band Rush produced a song called "Free Will." Their lyrics tell us that you still have made a choice if you decide to do nothing. For heaven's sake, rock stars get this right, yet entire societies seem to lack an understanding of these simple concepts.

Heaven knows that before I began my research, I lacked the understanding. Most people have come to believe rock stars consist primarily of pot smoking, drug-induced partiers chasing groupies. Ok, some do, but did you know that Brian May, the legendary guitarist of Queen, has a Ph.D. in astrophysics? His knowledge of physics was partly responsible for Queen's extraordinary sound. How about Gene Simmons of KISS? Well-known for a tongue that can probably clean out the bottom of a peanut butter jar, Simmons has a teaching degree. He dominated his competition when he participated in one of Trump's Apprentice TV episodes. Tom Morello of Rage Against the Machine has a BA in political science. That may be why they are considered one of today's most politically active bands.

Now, back to our regularly scheduled program. I go on little rants now and then. The point is that taking no action is still taking action.

Look at some leadership books or watch some leadership videos, and you will find a cornucopia of content telling us how leaders take action and how leadership is about knowing when to act and when not to act. Note that beliefs and actions do not require a person to be in any position in any hierarchy, nor does achieving success. However, taking or not taking any action leads to success or non-success. Success is our third component.

CHAPTER THREE

From Action to Success

Success

When asking people to define leadership, you will likely get hundreds of different answers. Ask a person to define success, and you will get a similar result. The complexity around the concept of success is staggering, with conflicting answers in direct contrast to one another. However, just like defining when a person acts in leadership, there is an answer.

Our definition of success comes from Earl Nightingale in his 1957 radio broadcast. Nightingale defines success as "the progressive realization of a worthy ideal."

Success is not about some end goal. Success comes from taking action or not taking action, and through a combination of unsuccessful and successful attempts, we continue to progress toward something. Success is an infinite journey toward whatever you decide is your worthy ideal. Small milestones, typically known as goals, can exist along that infinite journey.

In 1986, James P. Carse published a book, *Finite and Infinite Games*. Simon Sinek, who wrote *Start with Why* (2009) and *Leaders Eat Last* (2014), takes Carse's concept and produces another book, *The Infinite Game* (2019). What does Sinek tell us? We must treat businesses like an infinite game. The worthy ideal is to ensure that the business continues, no matter who holds any executive positions in the hierarchy. Along that infinite journey, sometimes we will succeed and sometimes fail. Life and business are both infinite journeys, a progression. Therefore, Nightingale's definition best describes the concept of success.

We also tend to use negative language that is counterintuitive to creating a *take-action mindset*. The term failure has a negative connotation. A denotation is a dictionary definition. A connotation is an idea or feeling that a word invokes in addition to its literal or primary meaning. Failure creates a negative feeling, causing a belief that continuing is pointless. Change the language and approach, and you change the mindset, which can lead to continued action. Thomas Edison expresses the concept of success in such a way.

> *I have not failed. I've just found 10,000 ways that won't work.* ~Thomas Edison

Edison was progressing toward a worthy ideal. Along that journey, he had successes and non-successes. Saying "other ways that won't work" does not have that same high level of negative connotation attached to it. That's the point of our definition of success. We don't fail. We experienced ways that didn't have the outcome we desired. We then gain insight from that outcome.

In Norman Vincent Peale's earlier quote, we see the same principle of how success is achieved when we do not get the desired outcome.

> *Action is a great restorer and builder of confidence. Inaction is not only the result, but the cause, of fear. Perhaps the action you take will be successful; perhaps different action or adjustments will have to follow. But any action is better than no action at all.* ~Norman Vincent Peale

As humans, our thought processes, our ability to reason, and our fear of what others think easily overpower our desire to take action. Why? Because people care more about not failing than about succeeding. Let me repeat that. *People care more about not failing because of what others will think than they do about succeeding.* Squelch that fear by changing your definition of success so you can continue progressing toward a worthy ideal.

Progressive has synonyms such as consistency, continuous, and growing, to name a few. Each of these labels has become an individual type of leadership, driving the rise in complexity. Success is a progression. Our newly discovered definition of success helps us to simplify defining when a person is acting in leadership.

Again, read some books on leadership or watch some videos. You will find that success is one of the central concepts consistently addressed. Look at the level of complexity, then try to define success. A common theme you'll notice is how "failure" is addressed. Leadership is about continuing and learning, whether we are successful or not in any endeavor, big or small. We use those experiences to gain insight. Once we can clarify and define success, everything else falls into place. Nightingale defined success for us. We experience ways that do not produce the desired outcome, and those experiences provide insight. Insight is our fourth component.

CHAPTER FOUR

Insight From Success

Insight

Knowledge is simply information, and actions are merely actions. What matters is the insight we gain from both the information and our actions.

> *There is nothing so terrible as activity without insight.*
> ~ Johann Wolfgang von Goethe

> *To understand another human being you must gain some insight into the conditions which made him what he is.* ~Margaret Bourke-White

To take action, whether reading to increase our knowledge or increasing our knowledge through taking action, when one does not intentionally use the insight gained from either, then you are just plowing without planting anything.

> *Insanity is doing the same thing over and over and expecting different results.* ~Unknown

Yeah, sorry. Albert Einstein never said that, but the value of that lesson cannot be overlooked. Insight only has value if we put it to use. Motivation without knowledge and insight is insanity.

> *Motivation alone is not enough. If you have an idiot and you motivate him, now you have a motivated idiot.* ~Jim Rohn

We gain knowledge. Putting that knowledge to work gives us experience. Those experiences lead to wisdom. Gaining a better understanding impacts our perception, awareness, intuition, comprehension, and judgment. Gaining a better understanding can be a worthy ideal. Isn't this what we say leaders do? They seek insight, correct? We act on that new insight, and our beliefs can be impacted. Are you beginning to see how this all ties together? We use the word insight because its definition hits the nail on the head. Insight is the capacity to gain an accurate and intuitive understanding.

> *Knowledge is knowing that a tomato is a fruit. Experience tells us that it does not taste good in a fruit salad. Wisdom is knowing not to put it in a fruit salad ever again.* ~Unknown

After covering four of the first five components, we can see the pattern that naturally occurs regarding synonyms. Beliefs encompass thoughts, mindsets, attitudes, opinions, and dispositions. Action covers work, effort, achievement, and endeavor. Progression encompasses developing, continuation, advancement, increasing, and growing. And now, insight covers wisdom, intuition, and judgment. We have now reached the fifth of the seven components of the BASIC Leadership blueprint: collaboration.

CHAPTER FIVE

Collaboration Activation

Collaboration

Collaboration has become one of the most overused buzzwords in recent decades and is one of the most made fun of concepts, keeping pace with humorous quips about leadership. We tend to think of collaboration as something that occurs between two or more people. This mindset is a short-sighted point of view.

In the movie *Master and Commander: Far Side of the World*, the doctor on the ship, Stephen Maturin, played by Paul Bettany, is also a naturalist—a biologist who primarily studies plants or animals.

During a conversation with the ship's captain, the doctor shares the fascinating attributes of a bug that disguises itself as a stick to confuse its enemies. Captain Jack Aubrey, played by Russell Crowe, takes and acts on that new insight. They disguise their warship as a vessel that hunts whales for profit. By doing so, they draw in their enemy and conquer them. While this may be a movie, collaboration with nature happens all the time in real life.

In 1928, Dr. Alexander Fleming returned from a holiday to find mold growing on a petri dish of Staphylococcus bacteria. He noticed that this mold was preventing the bacteria around it from growing. His studies showed that the mold produced a self-defense chemical that could kill bacteria. The name of that substance? Penicillin. The next time you visit your doctor for a prescription, you will know how that lifesaving drug came to be. Dr. Fleming collaborated with nature.

In Japan, many rice growers have begun using ducks as a natural way to produce healthier crops. The ducks feed on insects and weeds without eating or harming the rice plants. As the ducks swim, their paddle-shaped feet oxygenate the water and stir up the soil, and their droppings are a natural fertilizer—a win-win collaboration with nature.

One would think this is something new, but it is not. Collaborating with ducks was an ancient rice-growing practice replaced by chemicals and machinery as technologies advanced. Just as chemicals and machinery replaced the natural partnership with ducks, we see how a position in a hierarchy replaced leadership in its true essence. We can gain insight from rice growers, illustrating how we must return to the basics.

We can collaborate with others without ever being in direct contact with them. I collaborated with many people who have written about the concept of leadership. I did so without ever meeting them or having a discussion with them. You and I are constantly collaborating. You just gained a more accurate and deeper intuitive understanding of collaboration. You did so by collaborating with me through this book. Your beliefs have likely changed, and you will or will not act according to those new beliefs, allowing yourself to progress toward some worthy ideal.

> *If everyone is moving forward together, then success takes care of itself.* ~Henry Ford

> *Alone, we can do so little; together, we can do so much.* ~Helen Keller

> *Many ideas grow better when transplanted into another mind than the one where they sprang up.* ~Oliver Wendell Holmes

A plethora of collaboration quotes exist, from sports to business to life. Like Belief, Action, Success, and Insight, Collaboration consistently appears in many resources. It encompasses synonyms such as teamwork, alliance, cooperation, and joint effort.

We now have the first five of the seven components that provide the blueprint for acting in leadership. But how do they work together to create this blueprint?

CHAPTER SIX

BASIC In Motion - Wonkavator

BASIC is a Wonkavator

In 1971, the movie *Willy Wonka and the Chocolate Factory* was released. Mr. Wonka, played by Gene Wilder, is the eccentric, kooky, brilliant creator of the chocolate factory. Spoiler alert! At the movie's end, they enter a glass elevator, and Mr. Wonka says, "This is the great glass Wonkavator." Charlie's grandpa responds, "It's an elevator." Mr. Wonka corrects him and tells us, "It's a Wonkavator. An elevator can only go up and down, but the Wonkavator can go sideways and slantways, and longways, and backways, and squareways, and frontways, and other ways you can think of. Just press a button, and it takes you to any room in the factory." The first five components of the

BASIC Leadership blueprint work the same way as a Wonkavator.

When you've read as many books about platforms, theories, and systems as I have during my leadership studies, you run across diagram after diagram displaying circles, squares, and hexagons, generally arranged in a circle or oval.

Most of these diagrams have a common thread: They follow a specific pattern. They start at point A, then move to point B, then to C, D, E, and F. They put little arrows, sometimes with cool-looking arcs, that show where you go next.

They go in one direction. You cannot skip one component, jump across to some random element on the other side, or reverse. Or they have a two-option platform based on a yes or no answer to a question.

Those platforms lack flexibility. Now that I've pointed this out to you, it'll leap off the pages (or computer screen), grab your snout, and then squeeze it, making it honk like a clown nose. *Honk, honk.*

The BASIC leadership platform is a Wonkavator. You can move between the components based on what occurs naturally in any given situation. We've already experienced how this happens in the above explanations for each element.

For example, when you gain more insight, it can move you in one or more directions. Your beliefs can be confirmed or changed. New insight can drive you to collaborate with someone or something different. The new understanding can cause you to take more action, or it may help determine if a non-success or success is moving you toward a worthy ideal.

This structure allows for things to occur naturally. Most patterns are limited, restricting our ability to be innovative and creative. BASIC is a vital structure that defines when a person is acting in leadership. However, yes, there is almost always a "however." The primary outer ring components of the BASIC Leadership platform structure alone are insufficient for determining when a person is acting in leadership.

In the BASIC Leadership diagram, you may have noticed a central hub that you must pass through to move from one component to the next. This hub is the sixth component, integrity. It plays a crucial role in the BASIC Leadership blueprint, ensuring that all actions and decisions are guided by ethical principles. You'll see the image of the BASIC Leadership blueprint outer ring on the next page for reference.

Take note of the blank central hub We're going to give that a label.

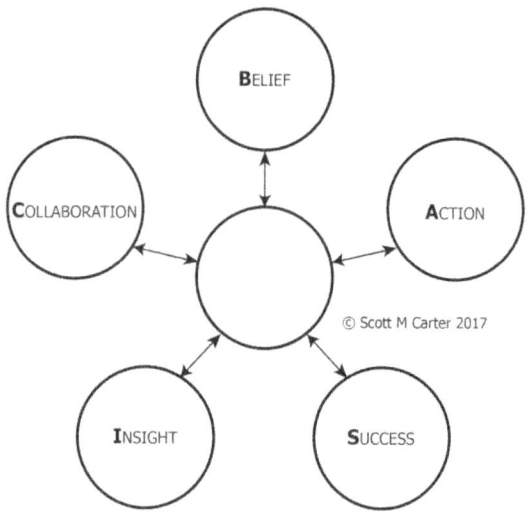

© Scott M Carter 2017

Back to BASIC™
Leadership Outer Ring

CHAPTER SEVEN

Integrity - Whole and Undivided

If someone asked you to explain the difference between values, principles, morals, ethics, and integrity, could you answer with a high degree of certainty? If you struggle, you are not alone. Most people struggle because these five things get jumbled, intermixed, and misunderstood.

In May 2018, Netflix released the *Cobra Kai* series, a spinoff 34 years after the *Karate Kid* movie trilogy. The Cobra Kai members live by a set of principles and values, as we all do. The members value "strike first, strike hard, no mercy." They operate under the principle of winning at all costs. The Cobra Kai are ok with any reputation bestowed upon them if they get to hold up the trophy to show they have won. They operate under that set of beliefs and chain of reasoning. When we watch the interactions in movies or mini-series like *Karate Kid* and

Cobra Kai, we have a natural sense of the contrast between right and wrong. To gain insight, let's examine the difference between values, principles, morals, ethics, and integrity.

- Values: 1. The regard that something is held to deserve; the importance, worth, or usefulness of something. 2. A person's principles or standards of behavior, one's judgment of what is important in life.
- Principles: A fundamental truth of position that serves as the foundation for a system of belief or behavior or a chain of reasoning.
- Morals: 1. Concerned with the principles of right and wrong behaviors and the goodness or badness of human character. 2. Holding or manifesting high principles for proper conduct.
- Ethics: 1. Moral principles that govern a person's behavior or the conducting of an activity. 2. the branch of knowledge that deals with moral principles.
- Integrity: 1. The quality of being honest and having strong moral principles; moral uprightness. 2. The state of being whole and undivided.

Choose One

Of the five choices above, which would you use as a test to determine if a person is acting in leadership? When we gain insight, the answer becomes clear. Our choice is integrity. Integrity becomes the sixth component and the hub of the BASIC Leadership blueprint, as shown in the image below.

When moving from one component to another using the Wonkavator approach, we will always pass through the integrity hub to determine if we are acting in leadership.

Real integrity is doing the right thing, knowing that nobody's going to know whether you did it or not. ~Oprah Winfrey

Integrity is doing the right thing when nobody's watching, and doing as you say you would do. ~Roy T. Bennett, The Light in the Heart

In looking for people to hire, you look for three qualities: integrity, intelligence, and energy. And if they don't have the first, the other two will kill you. ~Warren Buffet

Let's clarify a few things. Right and wrong are not subjective, and we know it. Because cannibals believe it is ok to kill and eat other human beings, it does not make that ritual valid. Cannibals eat people based on their values and principles. A person or society can act based on a set of principles or values and not act with integrity. Also, right and wrong are not based solely on legal or illegal. Just because something is legal does not make it moral. One can follow laws and still act without integrity.

I presented these five definitions in this order for a reason. Values and principles are about your beliefs and what is important to you. The actions of the Cobra Kai group provide an example of values and principles devoid of morals and integrity. Yet, in the series, people referred to the head of the Cobra Kai as their leader.

A sensei teaches students. The word sensei is a term of honor that translates to "teacher." It is an honor to help others learn because a sensei teaches students to be disciplined, accountable, and act with integrity. Forms of martial arts are not about how to hit people. The students are gaining wisdom on how to have discipline in their lives—a worthy ideal.

When a sensei acts with integrity, he or she is acting in leadership, thereby, a leader at that time. Or they can be a sensei who does not act in leadership. That's how easy it is to determine when a person is or is not a leader at any moment. A position, title, or placement in any hierarchy is entirely separate from leadership.

Do what you feel in your heart to be right – for you'll be criticized anyway. ~Eleanor Roosevelt

Humans get most of their exercise by jumping to conclusions, running off at the mouth, and pulling others down. Pulling others down is accomplished through criticism and judgment. Eleanor is known for many quotes that are rich with wisdom. We need more Eleanors in our world. Why not always act with integrity, since people will judge you no matter what you do? Acting in leadership requires a person to act with integrity.

CHAPTER EIGHT

Leadership Lifeline

A man sitting under a tree gets bonked in the head with an apple, and now we have orbiting space satellites. Partly true.

Isaac Newton watched an apple fall, but one never hit him on the noggin. Sir Isaac Newton, an English mathematician, physicist, and astronomer, lived when the amount of information available to people would be a drop of water in a fifty-five-gallon barrel compared to what is known today. Newton lived from 1643 to 1727. His insights are legendary. Newton showed us that for every action, there is an equal and opposite reaction.

Not long after Newton had left this world, Benjamin Franklin worked diligently to understand and harness the power of electricity. Historical accounts tell us it was around 1752. Teachers worldwide use the story of Franklin flying a kite during thunderstorms. An activity not recommended today because we have more insight into the dangers.

Together, Newton and Franklin help us understand that there is a balance in life. For example, electricity cannot exist without a positive side and a negative side. Would you want to throw out the negative side of electricity? Of course not. And if you tried, you'd fail because it's a built-in component of nature and the universe.

There must be an equal and opposite reaction to everything. Positive cannot exist without negative, and good cannot exist without evil. It's not that we want evil; without it, there would be nothing to contrast against to define what good means.

Negative is normal. It's part of life. We must learn to handle the negative. We do not ignore it; we deal with it. We handled it when we discussed the negative impacts of the word "failure" while defining success.

A gardener pays attention to the weeds in their garden. They know the weeds will come. They will have to deal with them, or those weeds will take over. Our lives are our garden, and we get to handle the weeds that infest it.

Nature, in so many ways, helps us to define leadership. Nature and the universe show us the way. The minute we are all born, life thrusts us into a battle between good and evil, darkness and light, negative and positive, Tierney and Freedom.

We are in that war, like it or not. The draft is automatic. No one is exempt. When goodness sleeps, guess who never sleeps? Evil. In the absence of light, darkness prevails. Guess who moves in if goodness does not arouse itself and becomes active? Evil. Positive and negative are organic. They exist naturally in our lives, in the universe. This differentiation between good and bad is what the leadership lifeline represents in the image below.

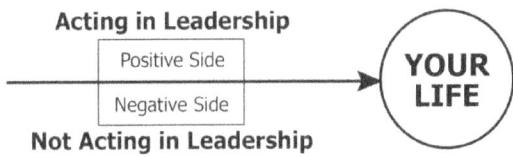

Leadership Life Line

© Scott M Carter 2017

Newton understood that for every action, there is an equal and opposite reaction. We must take action and gain insight from those actions to move toward the worthy ideal of living on the positive side of the leadership lifeline.

The universe's natural order tells us that the integrity hub filter itself is a great start. Many things can pass through the integrity filter because they do not violate acting with integrity, yet those things should not be any type of leadership. For example, eating too much and not exercising, which leads to being unhealthy, end up in long, drawn-out debates concerning right or wrong. A sumo wrestler needs to be significantly overweight to compete in that sport. Applying how a sumo wrestler eats to the integrity hub as a test of acting in leadership would not be effective. Beyond the integrity hub, how could we continue to answer the question, when is a person acting in leadership? The answer: The Leadership Lifeline.

Nothing in life is perfectly neutral. During our forward progression in life, we are on one side or the other on a horizontal line. We constantly move in and out of acting in leadership. Our goal is to progress toward acting in leadership more than not.

Leadership is an art, not a science. People have been trying to force a scientific formula like the gravitational acceleration constant of $g = 9.81$ m/s2. Acting in leadership is fluid, moving in many directions while attempting to remain on the positive side of the leadership lifeline.

> *If you can't explain it simply, you don't understand it well enough.* ~Albert Einstein

As I stated in the introduction of this book, the one you are reading right now, we are defining what it means to act in leadership. In my book, *There Is No Such Thing As Business Leadership*, I presented my arguments for why leadership is not a position in any hierarchy and how most of what is offered under the label of leadership is misguided.

If I take the time to present what leadership isn't, it stands to reason that I must illustrate what leadership is in its true essence. In the first eight chapters we reviewed the BASIC Leadership blueprint. The rest of this book encompasses arguments for why the BASIC Leadership blueprint tells us when we are acting in leadership. We will begin with how we are being propagandized to not act in leadership.

CHAPTER NINE

Propaganda

The word propaganda comes from the Latin verb propagare, which means to spread and promote an idea or theory as widely as possible. It also means to disseminate, communicate, or pass on.

There is nothing negative about the origin, the concept of propaganda, or its general existence. Propaganda is a consistent, enduring effort to create or shape events to influence the publics relation with an enterprise, idea, or group. What does that sentence mean in today's world? *Any form of marketing.* That's it.

The key questions should be to create or shape what? And for what purpose? Only then can a person begin to gain real insight as to whether it might be deemed positive or negative.

In 1928, Edward Bernays wrote a book on the subject, aptly called *Propaganda*. On page 52, Bernays states,

> *This practice of creating circumstances and of creating pictures in the minds of millions of persons is very common. Virtually no important undertaking is now carried on without it, whether the enterprise is building a cathedral, endowing a university, marketing a moving picture, floating a large bond issue, or electing a president. Sometimes the effect on the public is created by a professional propagandist, sometimes by an amateur deputed for the job. The important thing is that it is universal and continuous; and in its sum total it is regimenting the public mind every bit as much as an army regiments the bodies of its soldiers.*

Could you imagine an employment ad for your company titled, "Professional Propagandist," and a subheading that reads, "10 years of experience successfully influencing the masses using effective propaganda"? What pops into your head? A negative image?

I did not write this chapter to give you a history lesson on the word propaganda. This chapter aims to open your eyes to how you are being influenced, consciously and subconsciously, and how you are being manipulated through propaganda to "not act in leadership." Today, we call it marketing.

> *You are being manipulated through propaganda to "not act in leadership." Today, we call it marketing.*
> ~Scott M. Carter

The term "marketing" sounds really pretty and professional, and for some reason, the term hits most of us in a positive light. When we hear the word propaganda, negative images of wartime messages from the enemy or slanderous statements from politicians pop into our heads. Everything that comes at us today is propaganda. Now that we understand that, perhaps we will take notice, and only then will we avoid being influenced to do things that are the exact opposite of acting in leadership.

There have been movements to educate people on the tactics used when entities such as politicians or governments market to us and to spread and promote an idea or theory as widely as possible. It is propaganda from professional propagandists. Now, we give them titles such as Marketing Director, Public Relations Expert, Communications Coordinator, and a cornucopia of other creative wording that puts what propagandists do in a more positive light. *Do I have your attention yet?*

I'm not sure why, but it appears that we stopped teaching our youth how we are influenced and manipulated through propaganda, and we began teaching everyone to be propagandists.

> *It seems we stopped teaching our youth how we are influenced and manipulated through propaganda, and we began teaching everyone to be propagandists.*
> ~Scott M. Carter

The number of people who seek marketing degrees is staggering. No one wants a propagandist degree, yet they are the same. In my research, I found a video shown to high school juniors and seniors beginning in 1948. The focus of the film was to teach the techniques of propaganda.

In this particular film, they focused on strategies used by politicians. They presented examples of techniques such as glittering generalities, transfer, name-calling, card staking, testimonials, plain folk, and bandwagon.

What the film did not do was pick a political side. It was neutral. Fictitious candidates and no party affiliations were used in the examples. They simply illustrated the techniques all politicians used and how we are manipulated into voting one way or another. Imagine what elections would look like today if we taught our youth to think for themselves.

Today, the educators in our schools pick a political side and then teach students that this is the only viewpoint, turning students against one another, and teach kids to hate those who do not think exactly like they do. How sad that our society have gone backwards and teach people how *not to act in leadership.*

Once we understand what it means to act in leadership, we can then learn not to be so easily influenced to "not act in leadership." It comes at us from every angle under the guise of marketing when it is all *propaganda.*

CHAPTER TEN

Heart Disease, Stress, and Anxiety

Ever heard the phrase, "Stress, the silent killer?"

In 1973, a forty-year old man lay in a hospital bed thankful that he was still alive. He had just had a heart attack, a myocardial infarction.

A mere twenty minutes earlier, the warning signs began with a lack of ability to concentrate. He felt exhausted and experienced blurry vision. Then, like an elephant slowly lowering itself onto his chest, the pressure in his rib cage intensified. Two minutes seemed like a lifetime. That pain shot from his breastbone to his shoulders, neck, jaw, and down both arms.

He says he was lucky to have been in a hospital when this occurred. But what was he doing in a hospital in the first place? He was not there because he had a heart condition or because he was being treated for anything.

He was there because this man was a doctor and not just any doctor. That same morning, the morning he experienced a heart attack; this doctor gave a lecture on heart attacks and sudden death.

This same intensive care patient had accepted the position of Chief of Cardiology at the University of Nebraska one year earlier in 1972. His name? Robert S. Eliot, M.D.

A heart attack expert is now flat on his back in a hospital bed, looking at things from the patient's viewpoint—a life-changing event, to say the least.

Wait just a dog-gone-minute! The Chief of Cardiology at the University of Nebraska had a heart attack? Yes. An expert in the diseases of the heart and a heart specialist just had a near-death experience from the very thing he lectures on.

He did not show any signs of heart disease. He did not smoke, was not overweight, and did not have high blood pressure. What the heck was going on?

A substantial portion of people in the United States and now around the world still today do the very things that caused Dr. Eliot's heart attack. That's the bad news. The good news is that there is a solution. That solution has been around for a very long time; it's called acting in leadership.

Dr. Eliot tells us that his heart attack was the best thing that could have happened to him. And it was the best thing that could have happened for all of us when it comes to producing some of the science behind what constitutes acting in leadership.

Shortly after his heart attack, Dr. Eliot created the Life Stress Simulation Laboratory at the University of Nebraska Medical Center. The lab originated with an idea by one of Dr. Eliot's colleagues, James Buell. Together, working for over a year, they developed a practical and effective way to test the effects of stress on our cardiovascular system. They then built their new international headquarters, the Institute of Stress Medicine, in Denver, Colorado.

Dr. Eliot, along with eight medical experts and three editing experts, compiled sixteen years of research and put their findings into two books, *Is It Worth Dying For: How to Make Stress Work for You—Not Against You* (1984, 1989), and *From Stress to Strength: How to Lighten Your Load and Save Your Life* (1995).

Written based on scientific evidence and in simple language you and I understand, his research provides us part of the road map for acting in leadership.

Acting in Leadership

Most of the things we hear regarding what it means to be a leader must be corrected. That's a pretty darn bold statement to make. To be a leader, a person must act in leadership. I decoded the blueprint for what it means to act in leadership. We are being fed a lot of crap, and it's slowly killing us. And I am not talking solely about food.

According to the CDC, Centers for Disease Control and Prevention, heart disease is the leading cause of death for men and women in the United States. From 2018 to 2021, one person died every 33 seconds in the

United States from cardiovascular disease. Heart disease costs the United States about $239.9 billion each year in 2018 and 2019.

Stress and anxiety are slowly killing most of us. Not acting in leadership causes stress and anxiety. Learning to reduce both stress and anxiety is a component of acting in leadership.

Long before Dr. Eliot began his cardiovascular studies, nature knew what acting in leadership meant. Did you know that nature has put a pharmacy in our bodies? Nature's pharmacy tells us when we are acting in leadership.

CHAPTER ELEVEN

Nature's Pharmacy - The Bad

If a person walked up to you wearing a trench coat, a duster, the kind worn in gunslinger movies, slowly opened one side where a cornucopia of drugs sat in various pockets, and offered you some, let's say, heroin or cocaine or meth, would you take them? Of course not. Why?

Two reasons. First, they are bad for us and can kill us. Second, we have control over the choices we make in life. Your body is the trench coat-wearing drug dealer and you have some choices to make.

Nature has created a well-stocked pharmacy in our bodies, and we can control how much of those chemicals get dumped into our systems. Just like you can say no to the trench coat-wearing drug dealer on the street, you can say no to nature's pharmacy of chemicals that can slowly kill you.

Dr. Eliot learned this the hard way. He changed how he lived and he started acting in leadership using his own advice which he now gives to his patients and test subjects based on his research. Because he did so, at the time I wrote this chapter, Dr. Eliot was still alive at the age of 95.

Acting in leadership and not acting in leadership release chemicals into our bodies. Not acting in leadership slowly poisons your cardiovascular and immune systems.

> *Acting in leadership and not acting in leadership release chemicals into our bodies. Not acting in leadership slowly poisons your cardiovascular and immune systems.* ~Scott M. Carter

If you were asked what chemicals nature has put into our little personal pharmacies, could you name any? Just as important, what causes each one to be released, and what effect does it have on you? Don't feel bad; most people cannot.

Our actions and those of others cause the release of a multitude of chemicals into our bodies. We will gain insight into six natural chemicals: endorphins, dopamine, serotonin, oxytocin, cortisol, and adrenaline. The big Mac Daddy of all questions is, *why do these chemicals exist in the first place*? The answer? Nature helps us define when we are acting in leadership.

Cortisol.

Cortisol, the primary stress hormone, increases sugars (glucose) in the bloodstream, enhances your brain's use of glucose, and increases the availability of substances that repair tissues. I don't know about you, but I want my body to be able to repair tissue. We need cortisol.

However, there is always a yin and yang, a balance to life. Stress and anxiety release cortisol. Guess what happens if a person is always stressed out or anxious? Nature punishes us. Excessive amounts of this chemical damage our cells and can lead to things like cancer. That's a darn good reason to pay attention to stress and anxiety.

Our drug dealer, nature, may not ask for money when it divvies out cortisol, but there is always a price to pay. I find it fascinating how those who hold top-level positions in organizations assume that when a person is not stressed or anxious about missing a random arbitrary monetary goal, they think that person does not care.

Somehow, we equate stress and anxiety with caring, and even worse, we equate it with being a leader. Yet, what do we say that leaders do? They remain calm. Who should remain calm? All of us. Why? The chemical drip, drip, drip of cortisol from stress can kill us very slowly.

Society teaches us stress. It is a learned behavior. And we do it to ourselves based on propaganda. Ummmm, I mean marketing. We add activity after activity to our plates. The kids need to be in three sports. We need to work late and impress the boss. We need a huge house and a plethora of gadgets and toys, all of which require maintenance and take up space somewhere. I bought some new things, and I rarely use them because I don't have the time. Sounds silly. But that is what we do, and it all creates stress. Drip, drip, drip, the cortisol enters our bodies.

During my career, I have held the top position in different departments. In the latter part of my career, I frequently heard statements like, "You're always so calm no matter what happens." That wasn't always the case. I was a hothead when I was young. The smallest of things would set me off. I'd get mad at objects like the object did something to me and was at fault. I remember trying to attach a backrest and luggage carrier to my first motorcycle. When I struggled, I blew up, cursing the bike and the backrest, blaming those inanimate objects. And, of course, looking to the sky and blaming God.

Dr. Eliot and his team labeled those most at risk as hot reactors. I'll let you in on a little secret. The term "hot reactors" does not mean people who display anger in emotional outbursts, although it can include those people. Those most likely to do damage to themselves through stress and anxiety often do not show any of those emotional signs. The stress and anxiety happen inside, quietly.

I was one of those people. I looked calm, but I was still a candidate for releasing damaging amounts of cortisol into my body. And cortisol was not the only harmful chemical I was dumping into the only place I have to live my life, which is my body. Not only was the stress self-induced, but I also combined it with anger, releasing another chemical, adrenaline.

Adrenaline

FUD is an acronym for Fear, Uncertainty, and Doubt, coined by Dr. Elliot and his team. Have any of those three things in your life? If you said no, you're full of poopy. Live your life with high levels of FUD, and you're not acting in leadership.

> FUD – Fear, Uncertainty, and Doubt are killing you. You do not have to live that way. You can choose to act in leadership. ~Scott M. Carter

Adrenaline is responsible for your body's 'fight or flight' response. It helps you react quickly in a dangerous or stressful situation. Adrenaline is released when your brain perceives excitement, danger, fear, or a potential threat. We use the phrase "adrenaline junkie" to describe thrill seekers who jump out of planes and free fall before opening their parachutes. We should know nature provides a pharmacy in our bodies because we talk about being junkies.

If your adrenal glands produce too much adrenaline, it can cause high blood pressure from pheochromocytoma. There's a ten-dollar word. We can get bad headaches and high blood pressure from too much adrenaline, yet some self-induce through thrill-seeking. Adrenaline's true purpose is to keep us alive, to give us short bursts of extraordinary strength and energy for self-preservation. When we get angry, we release adrenaline, which should be reserved for self-preservation. Now, I choose not to get angry, to not self-induce with adrenaline.

CHAPTER TWELVE

Nature's Pharmacy - The Good

Dopamine

Dopamine is both a self-preservation and a reward chemical. Nature has created a "feel good" chemical that rewards us for setting and accomplishing goals. When you accomplish something such as planting and harvesting food, the result of completing that goal and all the little successes along the way release a shot of dopamine. Drip, drip, drip, yum, yum. In other words, taking action toward a worthy ideal where we experience success gets rewarded. That's pretty cool, folks. And, as always, too much of a good thing can be harmful.

Too much of this feel-good hormone can lead to negative behaviors like being overly competitive, aggressive, or having poor impulse control. Some people become addicted to eating, gambling, sex, drinking, or recreational drugs. Yes, even man-made drugs release drugs from nature's internal pharmacy. When the pendulum of dopamine swings too far one way, stress, anxiety, and even anger become the result.

Nature intended dopamine to be a good chemical. Not acting in leadership abuses this chemical.

Eat a yummy, not-so-good-for-you snack, then drip, drip, drip, you get some dopamine. Gamble and win, then drip, drip. I do it with my grocery lists. When I go to the store and find something I forgot to put on my list, I grab the item off the shelf, write it on the list, and cross it off. Drip, drip, give me some more of that. It's good stuff.

We get addicted to the little doses of dopamine that technology can create. People post something on a social media platform or send ten people a text, then wait for a like, comment, or response. The little beeps and dings of the text messages and notifications on our cell phones cause the drip, drip, drip of dopamine into our bodies.

We get addicted to the sounds our phones make. It's like we're out for Halloween and tricking people into giving us more candy. "Hey, look, I'm a pirate. Put some candy in my sack. Hey, I posted a selfie. Click the like button. Give me a shot of dopamine."

Then we do not get a response. No one likes our post. No one engages us on social media, we compare ourselves to others whom we have deemed influencers or as successful. Then comes anxiety, stress, depression, and anger. Now, nature hits us with some cortisol, causing damage to our bodies.

Nature designed dopamine as a reward to ensure we were motivated to survive. Surviving a day or week in modern times is not a real issue. Food is abundant and easily accessible except in third-world countries. We're not being chased by large animals or trying to hunt big game for their meat and skins.

Technology and an abundance of food in most countries mean we do not require many survival skills. Instead, not acting in leadership constantly drips dopamine into our bodies, which is harmful. We are tricking nature into giving us more drugs, like writing an illegal prescription at our local pharmacy, except our bodies have no law against doing so. Negative behaviors like being overly competitive, aggressive, or having poor impulse control work against acting in leadership.

Endorphins

Endorphins mask pain. Over the millennia, our bodies have developed many ways to help us survive. For a very long time, life was different than it is now, requiring hunting and gathering, long journeys, and abundant hardships. Nature knew this. During these challenging times, a hunter or traveler might be injured. Nature said, "Hey, I can help you to continue with less pain." Endorphin comes from the words "endogenous," which means within the body, and "morphine," an opiate pain reliever. Endorphins are a feel-good chemical because they can make us feel better and put us in a positive state of mind.

Our body releases endorphins when it feels pain and when we are stressed. Yay! Nature is helping us to counter that awful stress. We also get a shot of this good stuff during pleasurable activities such as exercise, massages, eating, and sex. The last one helps us to see why endorphins fit the self-preservation category. Sex leads to procreation, the continuation of our species.

Endorphins do not play as crucial a role as cortisol or dopamine, so why include it? There are two reasons. First, endorphin levels below the norm are responsible for mood deterioration, which is associated with a higher risk of depression and other affective disorders. Second, and more importantly, endorphins illustrate just how thorough nature has been when it comes to creating pharmacies in our bodies. Nature is so smart that it also gave us two collaboration chemicals.

Oxytocin

Our body releases oxytocin during childbirth and lactation to feed the newborn. Oxytocin also acts as a chemical messenger in your brain and plays a vital role in human behaviors. The first is the parent-infant bonding. Others include social interactions such as sexual arousal, recognition, trust, and romantic attachment.

Oxytocin is a chemical that provides the feeling we get from emotional bonds and physical touch. It's a collaboration chemical designed to reward us for the right behaviors. The effect of this chemical is why all the separation, social distancing, lockdowns, and masking during COVID-19 have had such adverse effects on society, leading to a rise in depression and suicidal attempts.

Oxytocin builds up slowly and stays in the system longer than adrenaline or dopamine. You can't get addicted to oxytocin. When we have oxytocin in our bodies, it reduces our susceptibility to things that cause addiction. For example, we can counter the addictive chemical dopamine. Because oxytocin builds up slowly, we say, "Trust takes time." We judge each other by the consistency of our behaviors, not just one or two events. Over time, we decide whether we trust someone.

Whether at work or in our personal lives, when a person violates the integrity hub and acts or thinks on the negative side of the leadership lifeline, then there is no oxytocin for anyone. We can kiss collaboration goodbye. This aspect of life is so important that nature doubled up on it.

Serotonin

Serotonin plays several roles in our bodies, including influencing learning, memory, and happiness, and regulating body temperature, sleep, sexual behaviors, and hunger. Fairly significant, wouldn't you agree?

When we feel the emotion of pride, that is because of the chemical serotonin. It's ok to have pride in a job well done, but it is not ok to be prideful. There is a difference.

Serotonin boosts our confidence and makes us feel fantastic. Why is public recognition so powerful? We get a shot of serotonin, those doing the recognition get a shot, and those seeing the recognition also get a shot of this beautiful chemical. That is how nature approached collaboration. Giving credit to others and sharing the credit with others creates a bond between people.

CHAPTER THIRTEEN

Nature, More Intelligent
Than All Of Us

What do you get when you cross a hunting dog with a telephone? A Golden Receiver. What do you get when you cross a chicken with a centipede? Enough drumsticks to feed an army. What do you get when you combine an elephant and a rhino? Elephino (El-if-I-know). That last one is what most people would say when you ask what chemicals nature provides in our bodies and why. Yeah, cheesy dad jokes. Suck it up, buttercup.

Dopamine has been linked to intrinsic motivation in goal accomplishment, whether academic, personal, or professional. Oxytocin is a collaboration chemical designed to reward us for the right behaviors. We get a shot of serotonin for giving recognition, and those who witness that act also get a dose.

We also get punished chemically for not acting in leadership. Stress and anger, mostly self-induced, can take years off of our lives by dumping excessive amounts of cortisol and adrenaline into our bodies.

All of these are leadership chemicals. They tell us when we are acting in leadership and when we are not acting in leadership. During my research I have found a pattern associated with calling one of these six "the leadership" chemical. Again, this was born out of associating leadership with a position in organizational hierarchies and doing business—a myth. Propaganda.

Nature did not say, "I will reward you for influencing others, inspiring others, or acquiring followers." Nature is more innovative than all of us combined regarding acting in leadership,

The damage that adrenaline and cortisol do to our bodies is insane. We pump them into our bodies in the name of leadership under misguided leadership labels, which sprung from attaching leadership to a position in a hierarchy and associating it with doing business. Then, we create what we think are solutions. Those so-called solutions are actually treatments for symptoms, rather than addressing the root causes.

Remember what we are doing here. I am illustrating how the BASIC Leadership platform defines when a person is acting in leadership and thereby being a leader only when acting in leadership. We will constantly, throughout our lives, move in and out of acting in leadership and being a leader minute by minute, hour by hour, and day by day.

This premise is very simple and very basic. If you are stressing yourself out, are you acting in leadership? If you are causing stress in the lives of others, are you acting in leadership? The answer to both is an easy "no."

At the time of his heart attack, Dr. Eliot did not have the luxury of the scientific knowledge we have now. He did, like many, have access to other information without scientific proof had he chosen to seek it.

After reading this book, which you are reading right now, you can no longer use ignorance as an excuse from either a scientific or philosophical standpoint.

In every chapter up until this one, the quotes used have been from more recent times—the mid-1800s and more recent. Where do you suppose those ideas, those concepts about beliefs, actions, success, insight, and collaboration might come from? How long have those *acting in leadership principles* and the lessons that teach us about them been around?

The answer is 2,500 years or more. Plato lived from 429 B.C. to 347 B.C., which is over 2,400 years before I wrote this book. He is one of many who tried to enlighten us on what it means to act in leadership and warn us about the effects of not acting in leadership.

> *Nothing in the affairs of men is worthy of great anxiety.* ~Plato, Timaeus

If asked, could you tell us what modern-day lessons does this quote from Plato teach us? For centuries, we have been provided the insight to address the root causes of things like heart disease. Dr. Eliot and his team gave us the scientific evidence to back up what it means to act in leadership when it comes to stress and anxiety. Perhaps now we will listen to those who came before him. They provided guidance for us all to be sagacious, have keen mental discernment, and have good judgment, which are just two of the many attributes of acting in leadership.

In his books, Dr. Elliot provides us this insight from his research.

> ➢ Stress may be the greatest single contributor to illness in the industrial world.
> ➢ The mind and body are interrelated
> ➢ You need to treat the mind and body

One of the most important things in that warning is the "mind and body" wording. We do more damage to ourselves due to our beliefs and the actions associated with those beliefs than anything else in life. Hold onto your seat. You are about to go on a leadership journey like none you have ever experienced.

CHAPTER FOURTEEN

History of Acting In Leadership - Insight

To get from one place to another in 450 B.C. was not easy. And that did not change much for thousands of years. In that era, what would it be like to travel from China to India, or Greece to China, or India to Greece? These travels could range from 3,592 miles to 4,371 miles, and that is as the crow flies.

What are the odds that philosophers in China collaborated with philosophers in Greece and India? Did the writings of philosophers in India make it to Greece? Did the writings of the philosophers in India make it to other places like Israel? And if they did, was there a language barrier? How many people could read and write? How many people could translate languages and do so effectively?

In the early 21st century, it would be easy for multiple countries to meet for some sort of summit or conference to discuss any subject. Not so much thousands of years ago.

In modern times, we zip around the planet in a matter of hours. What did travel and sharing ideas and philosophies look like 2,500 years ago, 1,500 years ago, or even 500 years ago?

Different languages, mostly travel by foot on land, horse and cart if you were of wealth or high societal status, and perhaps by boat for the sea-faring coastal societies.

In the next four chapters, we will look at the philosophies of cultures, thousands of miles apart, but relatively close in time lines. These societies provide the insight into how the writings of the most prominent philosophers all mirror one another and provide us with the templates for acting in leadership.

In our modern era, the philosophies of India, China, Greece, and the *Bible* have been studied in great detail. Because we now have so much insight into the teachings of these past cultures, I have been able to assemble the blueprint for acting in leadership.

Semantic Tree Learning

Most people recognize the name Elon Musk. Musk co-founded the electronic payment firm PayPal, and in 2002, founded SpaceX, a company that makes rockets and spacecraft. He was a major early founder of Tesla, which makes electric cars and batteries, and became its chief executive officer in 2008. Most recently, he purchased the social media platform Twitter.

Do you know one Musk's techniques for remembering things? It is a simple method that allows him to easily link complex ideas together. It's called "Semantic Tree Learning." In short, it's about starting with an intuitive understanding of the basics, the foundational principles that allow a person to connect an abundance of small details together to make sense of them all.

Picture a large oak tree. The trunk of the tree and the largest branches are the foundational principles. You look at those first. There is only one trunk and a handful of large branches. Only after you understand the trunk and large branches, which represent the foundational principles, you then look at the smaller branches and leaves, which represent the smaller details. Without the trunk and large branches, there is nothing for the leaves to hold onto.

You begin with the basic ideas or core truths, the big trunk and large branches of the tree, before getting to the leaves, the small, detailed parts. This technique allows you to link complex ideas to their simple foundational principles.

He says we try to learn by doing the opposite. Most people start by memorizing small facts and tiny details. Semantic tree learning is different from memorizing facts and small details.

The BASIC Leadership blueprint can be used in a comparable manner. The five outer ring components are the trunk of the tree and its large branches. Now, we will begin looking a bit further into the branches and the leaves of the mighty oak tree of acting in leadership.

Make sure you understand the fundamental principles, ie the trunk and big branches, before you get into the leaves, the details, or there is nothing for them to hang on to. ~Elon Musk

CHAPTER FIFTEEN

History of Acting In Leadership - Buddha

Some people transcend humanity. Buddha is one of them. Buddha was born Siddhartha Gautama, in what is now present-day Nepal, India. He lived from 563 B.C. to 483 B.C. and was a philosopher and teacher who started a movement called Buddhism.

Buddhism focuses on inner peace and wisdom, meditation, and morals, and enlightens us on concepts such as Karma, a Sanskrit word meaning "action, the effects of that action, which lead to an outcome." Karma is not about you getting revenge because someone wronged you.

The teachings of Buddha are extremely simple. Buddhism is based on what are known as the four noble truths. First, the truths are not noble. A person who understands them and applies them acts noble. Noble has two definitions.

1) belonging to a hereditary class with high social or political status; aristocratic, and
2) having or showing fine personal qualities or high moral principles and ideals.

The second definition applies to the four truths. Nobility is not about being superior to your fellow man. It's about the progression of becoming a better version of your former self.

The Four Truths

The first truth, known as Dukka, has two components. First, it tells us that every single one of us will suffer through things such as being born, experiencing sickness of some sort throughout our life, and we will die. These are unavoidable sufferings. For most people, nothing new or unknown about unavoidable things that might cause suffering.

Dukka tells us we will also suffer from encountering the unpleasant, separating from the pleasant and not gaining what we desire. What we consider unpleasant and pleasant are all tied to our perceptions, beliefs, experiences, and level of awareness. These types of suffering are self-inflicted and avoidable.

The second truth, known as Samudaya, provides the origin of these sufferings related to separation from the pleasant, and not gaining what we desire based on cravings, attachment, and negative actions.

Killing, stealing, and lying are basic negative actions that are brought on by desire, hatred, greed, and ignorance. Unlike birth, unavoidable illnesses, and death, actions such as murder, stealing, and lying cause avoidable suffering. Also, nothing complicated about this.

The third truth, known as Nirodha, is a combination of cessation and nirvana. Cessation is the process of ending or being brought to an end. Nirvana means to become distinguished, to blow something out, to remove it. Therefore, the third truth is about understanding what causes the self-inflicted suffering and also about understanding that we should stop doing the things that cause the suffering. In short, we understand that we should not do those things. Again, this is an extremely easy concept to grasp.

The fourth truth, known as Magga, is the path. In other words, how to accomplish cessation and nirvana. The third truth tells us we must remove what causes the suffering, and the fourth truth is the path to accomplish that, which is how to achieve cessation and nirvana. The following four bullet points are the trunk and large branches of the oak tree. Once we know these simple principles, we can quickly and easily link any small idea back to them. Semantic Tree Learning at its best.

- Dukka – Life contains suffering. Some unavoidable, some self-inflicted and avoidable.
- Samudaya – The origins of the self-inflicted suffering.
- Nirodha – We possess the ability to end self-inflicted suffering and should do so.

- Magga – The path to removing the self-inflicted suffering.

The four truths tell us what will happen to all of us. We are born, we will experience sickness, and eventually die. No one can avoid these. Beyond those inevitable things, our beliefs and actions will cause all other forms of suffering, and those will be self-inflicted or inflicted upon others, or both.

However, those sufferings are avoidable. When we gain insight, which is an intuitive understanding of what we do to cause them, we can progress toward the worthy ideal of the process of ending that self-inflicted suffering. Physical pain is inevitable; suffering is optional.

When we follow the path, then we are acting in nobility; we act in a noble manner. In their most simple form, those are the four noble truths and the teachings of Buddha.

To intentionally reduce our own self-inflicted suffering and not cause others to suffer is to act in leadership.

Sitting on my desk in front of me is a book, *The Four Noble Truths*, by Ven. Lobsang Gyatso. Gyatso goes into detail, expanding out into the branches and the leaves. Next to that is another book, *The Dhammapada* by Eknath Easwaran.

The Dhammapada presents Buddha's lessons connected to the four truths. It consists of twenty six chapters, all broken out into verses or lines numbered from 1 to 423. It is simple and easy to understand, and you can take any detailed item within it and tie it back to the four noble truths. What we see in the details, the verses, which represent the leaves of the tree, are the principles and lessons of acting in leadership.

Does anger cause suffering? Absolutely. In chapter eleven, we learned that anger dumps large amounts of adrenaline and cortisol into our systems.

Does anger ever solve anything? The answer is no. Anger clouds our judgment. We think more clearly when we are calm. This is a modern-day leadership trait. Remain calm and think clearly to come up with a solution.

One of my favorite scenes in *Star Wars: Revenge of the Sith* is when Anakin and Obi-Wan battle it out on some hot, molten planet. Obi-Wan says, "It's over, Anakin. I have the high ground."

It is true that the physical high ground can be an advantage in a battle, but this was a battle of good versus evil. Obi-Wan represented the moral high ground. He thought clearly and wanted to end the fight. Anakin's anger clouded his judgment, leading to severed limbs and a scorched body.

> *Give up anger, give up pride, and free yourself from worldly bondage. No sorrow can befall those who never try to possess people and things as their own.*
> ~ Buddha, *The Dhammapada*[1]

Chapter seventeen of the Dhammapada enlightens us on anger, pride, and blame, contrasting them with things on the positive side of the leadership lifeline. Why do we get angry? Because we choose to. Can we control our own anger? Yes, and those methods have been around for thousands of years.

Buddhism addresses all the leadership traits we discuss in today's societies, none of which involve a position in any hierarchy.

Anger is one of the leaves of the mighty oak tree when it comes to acting in leadership. We will look at more leaves as we work our way through what it means to act in leadership. For now, we're going to use the concept of anger to show alignment for how multiple cultures from thousands of years ago all understood the part anger plays when it comes to acting in leadership.

History of Acting In
Leadership - Lao Tzu

Lao Tzu lived in the 6th century B.C. Estimates put him around 571 B.C., in the middle of his life.

Best known as the author of the classic *Tao Te Ching,* or *The Book of the Way and its Power*, Lao Tzu is believed to be an older contemporary of Confucius and the founding figure of Taoism in China. That means when you read Chinese proverbs, he may have played a part in those foundational principles. Not fortune cookies, either. Those are American inventions that did not come from China.

One of the main ideas of Taoism is the belief in balancing forces, referred to as the yin and yang, illustrated in the symbol below. It's the positive and negative side of the leadership lifeline.

The yin-yang of life represents light and dark, hot and cold, action and inaction, good and evil—the universe's natural order. The yin is black; the yang is white.

You'll notice that each side has a small circle of the corresponding color of the opposite side. This correlation between good and evil shows how each side carries the seed or essence of the other. It tells us that these forces must coexist. One side cannot exist independently without the other. A person can never achieve being completely good or perfect. A little bad will always surface. Conversely, no one is completely bad; down deep, some good exists. The overall shape of the symbol also shows us how things flow together and are in constant change.

Taoism, also known by the name Daoism, is comprised of 4 teachings.

1) Simplicity, Patience, and Compassion
2) Going With The Flow
3) Letting Go
4) Harmony

Tao means a road, the path, the way. The way in which one does something; a method, doctrine, or principle that defines a philosophy. Te means virtue. Ching means a classic book. Therefore, Tao Te Ching is a book about living a virtuous life, one of integrity on the positive side of the leadership lifeline.

When we compare the four bullet points of Taoism to Buddhism, we see the alignment with the four noble truths. Letting go and going with the flow tell us that anger is the wrong reaction to things in our lives. When we allow anger to move in, we are out of harmony.

> *Excellent warriors are not violent.*
> *Excellent soldiers are not furious.*
> *Excellent conquerors do not engage.*
> *Excellent leaders of people lower themselves.*
> ~Lao Tzu, *Tao Te Ching*[1]

This Tao Te Ching passage tells us that even when we go into battle, anger puts us at a disadvantage. This principle is the message in the Star Wars fight scene between Anakin and Obi-Wan. Anger never serves us; it diminishes us in many ways. This passage tells us anger causes us to engage when we know we should not react.

Because of the language, we think this passage pertains to an army of soldiers all dressed in battle armor. It's a metaphor. We use metaphors to make the abstract concrete and relatable. People end up taking passages from the Dhammapada and the Tao Te Ching in a literal sense. These passages are designed to provide the principles and teachings of acting in leadership. Sometimes, these teachings show us the big picture; sometimes, the intricate details.

We can tie the warrior metaphor back to the trunk concepts of patience and letting go. We can also tie it back to the trunk foundation of Buddhism, the four noble truths.

Acting in anger produces regret. Regret is a form of suffering, and it is self-inflicted because we choose to act a certain way. That is just one of the many ways the little leaves of the mighty oak are all connected in one way or another.

History of Acting In Leadership - Socrates, Plato, and Aristotle

In the 1989 movie *Ted and Bill's Excellent Adventure*, a man from the future brings Ted and Bill a time-traveling phone booth.

Ok, a phone booth is a glass box 3 ft x 3 ft x 7 ft tall. By 1970, a person could not walk through most towns, even small ones, and not stumble upon this marvel of technology on the corner of some highly traveled street. One side of the booth has a bi-fold door, like you might see on a small closet. You can awkwardly squeeze into the booth through this door. And inside of it? A phone that connected you to other phones.

This glass display case, which presents you to the public like an imprisoned insect in a jar, is where Superman transformed from Clark Kent into his man of steel outfit. Odd choice, huh? A glass box doesn't conceal much.

I sit with a delightfully devilish grin on my face because somewhere in the future a person will have to explain what a cell phone is after it has become obsolete. Perhaps it will be replaced by eye glasses or a skull temple implant for what now seems commonplace. Such is the way of technological advancements.

In this time-traveling phone booth, Ted and Bill bring back historical characters such as Abraham Lincoln, Joan of Arc, and, of course, Socrates so he can teach them about what? His philosophies about how to act in leadership.

Socrates lived from 470 B.C. to 399 B.C., reaching the incredible age of 71. Pretty dang good for those times. Plato was a student of Socrates and lived from 429 B.C. to 347 B.C., exceeding Socrates' longevity by eleven years to the age of eighty-one. Aristotle was a student of Plato and lived from 384 B.C. to 322 B.C.

This sequence of teacher-student relationships becomes relevant because Socrates wrote down very little. All that is known about him has been inferred from accounts by others, including Plato, Aristotle, and historians who recorded quotes and speeches.

The fact that Socrates did not write much is common in historical accounts. Jesus did not write anything, either. Jesus taught acting in leadership, and many of his twelve disciples recorded his teachings. Then, others continued to write different variations of the lessons taught.

Socrates, Plato, and Aristotle also learned from others who preceded them. For instance, the seven sages, labeled as the wise men, played a part. Greek philosophers before and after Socrates were influenced by the Delphic maxims, a set of moral precepts inscribed on the Temple of Apollo in the ancient Greek precinct of Delphi.

That temple contained 147 maxims. A maxim is a short, concise statement expressing a general truth or rule of conduct. In today's world, we use "quote" rather than "maxim." You have probably seen a Greek maxim but have not known it by that name. Examples include "Know thyself," "Control Anger," and "Nothing to Excess."

Plato's works consist of his Fifty-Five Dialogs and Twelve Epistles. We saw an example at the end of chapter thirteen. Timaeus is one of Plato's Dialogs.

Nothing in the affairs of men is worthy of great anxiety. ~Plato, Timaeus

In the mid-seventeen hundreds, Floyer Sydenham began translating to English, completing nine of the dialogs, and Thomas Taylor translated the remainder. It's a five-volume set printed by R. Wilkes and sold by Jeffrey and Evans in 1804. *Very rare* and *very expensive* is the best way to describe this five volume set. I own a lot of books, but I do not own any of those books.

Greek philosophy runs deep and rich in context. Many historians focused on compiling and recording the early philosophies.

For example, Diogenes Laertius wrote a series of books called *The Lives of Eminent Philosophers*, which were known for helping to develop the concept of cynicism. He lived at the same time as Plato. Cynicism is an inclination to believe that people are motivated purely by self-interest and skepticism. Plato knew of Diogenes and had an opinion on his versions of what Socrates taught.

In the 5th century AD, Joannes Stobaeus compiled a valuable series of extracts from Greek authors. The work was initially divided into two volumes, each containing two books. Stobaeus' works detail the 147 maxims.

Buddhism and Taoism both have what I refer to as a leadership operating manual, the *Dhammapada* and the *Tao Te Ching*, whereas not so much when it comes to Greek philosophy. This complexity is why I went into more detail about Greek philosophy.

Where do we think the quotes of Lao Tzu, Buddha, Socrates, Plato, and Aristotle come from? Someone wrote them down. What do the Greek philosophers say about anger?

We can begin with one of the 147 maxims. "Control Anger," then go deeper if a person chooses to do so. You'd find a cornucopia of writings from Aristotle on Anger.

CHAPTER EIGHTEEN

History of Acting In Leadership - Jesus & The *Bible*

What is the best-selling book of all time? The *Bible.* No one has the exact number, but according to the research done by the British and Foreign Bible Society in 2021, somewhere between five and seven billion copies have been produced and distributed. Yes, that is a billion with a "b." The question is, why?

In my opinion, it teaches us how to act, how to behave. I will take that a step further and say that it teaches us to act in leadership, presenting the same messages and principles as Taoism, Buddhism, and Greek philosophy.

So much of the poetry, music, plays, operas, movies, and books of hundreds of years contain the lessons and principles presented in the *Bible*. This isn't about how religious a person is or isn't or whether a person believes in any sort of deity, a supernatural God, or a higher power. Remove that aspect for a minute and look at the lessons within.

We talked about Buddhism and Taoism both having what I would refer to as a leadership operating manuals, presented as the Dhammapada and the Tao Te Ching. The *Bible* is also a leadership operating manual. Filled with incredible stories, adventures, and precise guidance, it's not a wonder that so many people share it with others.

Other similarities exist as well. The Ten Commandments are the biblical equivalent of the maxims on the temple of Apollo. They teach how to act in leadership. "Thou shalt not kill" mirrors the Greek Delphi maxim "Shun murder."

Let's continue with the same theme as the previous three chapters. There are a multitude of passages in the *Bible* about anger, both its causes and the remedies—so many that I could write several lengthy chapters delving into the subject.

> *The acts of the flesh are obvious: sexual immorality, impurity and debauchery; idolatry and witchcraft; hatred, discord, jealousy, fits of rage, selfish ambition, dissensions, factions and envy; drunkenness, orgies, and the like. I warn you, as I did before, that those who live like this will not inherit the kingdom of God.*

But the fruit of the Spirit is love, joy, peace, forbearance, kindness, goodness, faithfulness, gentleness and self-control. Against such things there is no law. ~Galatians 5:19-23 (NIV)[1]

The Apostle Paul wrote Galatians. We see a multitude of things that all fall on the negative side of the leadership lifeline and the things that fall on the positive side of the leadership lifeline in direct contrast.

Anger is written as "fits of rage" and contrasted with the attributes of peace and kindness. These same messages, contrasting positive versus negative, exist across the different cultures we've discussed in the last three chapters.

Almost every major concept that we discuss in 2024 in relation to leadership is built into all of the cultures, all thousands of miles apart and all thousands of years ago. All of it is applied to us on an individual level and is not designed to be applied solely to a position in a hierarchy.

CHAPTER NINETEEN

Quotes, Maxims, Sources, Context & Meaning

Ever wonder if a quote or source is factual? Ever struggle with knowing if the context in which it is used is correct? Yeah, me too. We see many variations of the same lessons, which might cause confusion. It is important not to lose sight of the overall lessons of acting in leadership because of the source of the quote. Let me give you a modern-day example using music.

Have you ever wondered why so many albums sound better, or at least different than a live performance by a band or artist? Yes, the acoustics in the recording studios versus the large auditoriums and other factors make up some of the difference. However, for many studio recordings, the people who play the instruments are different from the people who play the instruments at a live performance.

Guitarists Danny Kortchmar and Waddy Wachtel, drummer Russ Kunkel, bassist Leland Sklar, and guitarist Steve Postell perform music specifically in recording studios. They are known as *The Immediate Family*, a unique group of iconic musicians who have played together for decades but not as their own band.

They have recorded with Hall-of-Fame artists such as Linda Ronstadt, James Taylor, Keith Richards, Stevie Nicks, Jackson Browne, Carole King, and Crosby, Stills, Nash & Young.

Even though the studio recordings may not be performed by the same band members who play on stage, it does not change the music's impact on us.

If I asked you who wrote the songs in the following list, you'd likely answer with the names listed along with the song.

- Dude (Looks Like a Lady) – Aerosmith
- Bad Medicine – Jon Bon Jovi
- You Give Love a Bad Name – Jon Bon Jovi
- I Hate Myself For Loving You – Joan Jet & The Blackhearts
- Inside Your Heaven – Carrie Underwood
- Livin' La Vida Loca – Ricky Martin
- Up On The Roof – James Taylor
- A Natural Woman – Aretha Franklin
- The Locomotion – Grand Funk Railroad
- Go Away Little Girl – Donny Osmond

You would be wrong if you agreed with the names that follow each song. Those are the bands or individuals who performed those hits. Desmond Child wrote or co-wrote the first six songs on the list, and Carole King wrote or co-wrote the last four. Child and King created some or all of the words, lyrics, and music for many songs from a long list of successful bands and singers.

If any of those hit songs are ones you really like, does the fact that Desmond Child or Carole King wrote or co-wrote them change how you feel about those songs? The answer is, "no." If you like a song, you sing along, making you feel good. It should change nothing.

Now, let's approach lessons in leadership from the same perspective. Have you ever seen the following quote?

> *Give a man a fish and you feed him for a day. Teach him how to fish and you feed him for a lifetime.*

Notice that I did not attribute that quote to anyone. When you search, especially on the internet, the World Wide Web, the Chinese philosopher Lao Tzu is often given credit. I could find no such reliable source to verify it belonged to Lao Tzu, nor could other researchers. However, there are different variations of this quote floating around.

For example, the following passage is found on page 342 of Anna Isabella Thackeray Ritchie's novel *Mrs. Dymond*, published in 1885.

> *He certainly doesn't practise his precepts, but I suppose the Patron meant that if you give a man a fish he is hungry again in an hour. If you teach him to catch a fish you do him a good turn. But these very elementary principles are apt to clash with the leisure of the cultivated classes.*

In many of Ritchie's works, she interestingly used old folk stories to depict modern situations and occurrences. Those tales included *Sleeping Beauty, Cinderella, Beauty and the* Beast, and *Little Red Riding Hood*. Like the fish analogy, they are meant to teach us lessons. Lessons about acting in leadership.

We find evidence that Ritchie provides us with a variation of it. Now I have another question for you. Like the songs of some of our favorite bands and artists, does it matter that Lao Tzu may not have said those exact words? The answer is both yes and no.

First, yes, with respect to adequately sourcing and attributing quotes and understanding their context and intent. We must always do our due diligence before referencing any source.

Second, no. Just because Lao Tzu may not have actually said it, that does not change the lesson being taught.

More recent sources, such as the authors from the New Thought Movement of the early 1900s and the Personal Development Movement of the late 1900s, are much easier to verify. Not so much as we go back in time. It is imperative to understand quotes, maxims, sources, and context, but more importantly, that we keep sight of the overall life lessons that have been understood for thousands of years.

Quotes or maxims are almost always part of a more extensive dialog. It is essential for you, the reader, to know this so you can locate and dig into the larger context if you choose to gain more insight.

For instance, the *Tao Te Ching* consists of 81 parts, often called chapters. Each chapter contains multiple verses. Each of those chapters looks much like prose or a poem. A chapter is a group of verses comprised of maxims, which are short, concise statements related to the presented lessons.

Buddhism works the same way. The original writings are called the *Dhammapada*, just as the original works of Taoism are called the *Tao Te Ching*. The translations are broken into parts or segments and assigned verse numbers. Different translators may use different words.

Greek quotes get a bit more challenging since there is not one book or original source. However, when one takes the time to dig into it, finding who and what to credit is possible. This complexity is why, in this book, you will experience a wide variety of Greek quotes that do not have the names of Socrates, Plato, and Aristotle attached to them. We're focusing on the lessons for acting in leadership, not a history lesson on those three people.

Similarly, much of the *Bible* is broken into verses, often used as quotes or maxims. *Bible* quotes can come from the NIV, New International Version, the KJV, the King James Version, the ESV, the English Standard

Version, NLV, the New Living Translation, and other versions. These are not different Bibles; they are different variations of the translation of the Bible, often translated centuries apart.

These variations are why it can be confusing when we see *Bible* quotes with the same verse numbers but different wording. For instance, the quote from the previous chapter, Galatians 5:19-23 (NIV), will likely have different wording depending on which version of the *Bible* translation a person finds.

That can lead us to think someone misquoted something. The message is the same, but the wording changes a bit depending on who translated it and when.

It's like having a conversation with a person. You say, "I love the song Bad Medicine by Bon Jovi." Then the other person says, "Bon Jovi didn't write it; Desmond Child did." And you're staring at them, thinking, "Where did that come from?" The conversation has been derailed. We derail the lesson by talking about some little leaves out on some distant branch of the tree.

Jesus preached a sermon on the mount and a sermon on the plain. There were no cameras or audio recorders. Imagine trying to remember what was said or imagine several people writing it down from memory hours or days later. In the case of those two sermons, Matthew helped Jesus write them, but they had to be translated. That's another area where we might see variations in the wording and phrasing, but the underlying messages are the same.

Whether it is Taoism, Buddhism, Greek Philosophy, or the *Bible*, they all address the same principles: virtue, evil, doubt, fear, hate, love, desire, greed, pride, the self, ignorance, intelligence, knowledge, understanding, wisdom, joy, pleasure, anger, and on and on. They cover a wide range of positive versus negative concepts, all of which teach us lessons for acting in leadership and not acting in leadership.

Imagine working within the expansive English language, deciding whether a specific Chinese, Indian, Greek, or Hebrew word should be translated to virtue, ethics, value, principle, or integrity. You had better have a darn good translator who understands the context. Even then, that translation will be subject to that person's experiences and beliefs.

Did you know that Buddha also did sermons? Yep, he taught and preached at different venues, just as Socrates, Plato, and Aristotle did.

I guarantee you that their wording and phrasing will differ when any person preaches the same message at multiple venues. The message will be the same, but the wording and phrasing will change.

Ask anyone who has ever given a lecture multiple times on the same topic. Those presentations would differ if you compared the videos, but the message is still the same. Are you starting to see the big picture yet?

Are these religions or philosophies? This question has been asked for a very long time. The reality is that the label is irrelevant. Call it what you like. They all contain the lessons of acting in leadership.

I learned the lesson of complexity and uncertainty of quotes the hard way. You can avoid self-inflicted suffering. If the quote you have, the book you have, or whatever it is you have been using or will be using to gain insight and to begin acting in leadership likely teaches the same lessons I present here in this book.

Do not throw out what you have or think some resource you have is incorrect because the quote, verse, or maxim does not match what you see here. There can be many variations, and those variations teach the same lessons when used in the correct context. If you understand the context and the lesson, then that quote or maxim will lead you down the correct path in life.

I do not claim that the quotes or maxims I use are the only ones, nor the best ones. I needed to choose sources to make my point about what constitutes acting in leadership. I chose to take the time to source what I present in this book. I did not take that same level of care in my previous books.

Metaphors, Parables, and Analogies

Last, but not least, for thousands of years, the lessons of acting in leadership were taught and understood using metaphors, parables, and analogies. Let's gain some insight.

> Metaphor; a thing regarded as representative or symbolic of something else, especially something abstract.

> Parable; a simple, usually short, fictitious story that illustrates a moral attitude or a religious principle.

Analogy; a comparison between two things, typically for the purpose of explanation or clarification.

In my last book, I wrote an entire chapter on how we still speak in metaphors today. We say, "Time is money." It takes the abstract concept of time and relates it to something concrete like money. We try to save time. One cannot actually do that, but we know what it means. We want to be more efficient by doing the same process in less time.

Parables have been used since people began to communicate. Writing and reading were not common place for thousands of years. People told stories to communicate many things, including the lessons of life. These parables use animals we associate with being clever (fox), stubborn (ass/donkey), timid (mouse), etc.

Analogies are much like metaphors. They convert an abstract concept into something we can better understand. Analogies use animals and nature to make the point. What we plant in our garden is what grows. Plant a poisonous type of nightshade and it will grow. Plant a healthy vegetable, and it will grow. Our minds, like a garden, will give back what we plant. Plant negative thoughts and negative actions will be the result.

Saying that leadership is _____ (fill in the blank with any of the hundreds of current definitions) is like rearranging the deck chairs on the Titanic. It solved nothing while the ship continued to sink. That's an example of an analogy.

People retain information when things rhyme or when things are short and simple. People knew this thousands of years ago. Therefore, they wrote lessons in short verses, in rhymes, and what we now know to be maxims.

When we read a few quotes or verses from Greek philosophers, the *Dhammapada*, the *Tao Te Ching*, or the *Bible*, and then get some context of the lesson being taught, that allows us to learn quickly, not to become bored or disinterested, and not become confused due to a high level of complexity. That's the power of the way the lessons of acting in leadership have been presented for thousands of years: metaphors, parables, analogies, maxims, short verses, and rhymes, sometimes in a poetic style.

Context and Interpretations

The number of ways we can say or express something has increased exponentially. Synonyms in the English language are one example.

> Synonym; *a word or phrase that has the same or almost the same meaning as another word or phrase in the same language*

Lists of synonyms are expanding at an incredible rate, and it's raising the level of complexity when it comes to the actual context of very simple lessons that have been around for thousands of years.

The context, the intended purpose, is of utmost significance. For example, in Chinese, one symbol is used to describe many things, and the way it is used determines its meaning. Therefore, when digging into the Tao Te Ching, it is necessary to read multiple interpretations of the lessons. I have done so in my research to determine context.

Here's a great example of a misinterpreted context. We learned that the Ten Commandments, like the sayings on the temple of Apollo, are maxims. One of the Greek maxims is "Shun Murder." Experts now say that the biblical commandment "Thou shalt not kill" should be "Thou shalt not murder." This biblical lesson can be easily misinterpreted if a person does not know the proper context of the word kill. Its more accurate context is about murder.

If a person is defending themselves in a life-threatening situation, and they end up killing the person who attacked them, they killed, they did not murder. Murdering someone is entirely different. I will do my best to ensure I get the context right, so you the reader, gain insight. Insight: *The Capacity to Gain an Accurate and Intuitive Understanding.*

Concepts like happiness, joy, and contentment can get confusing when someone does not understand the context. Happiness can mean the temporary state caused by a pleasurable or satisfying experience. Buying something you like can make you happy. You experience the temporary emotion of happiness. Happiness can also mean a state of well-being or contentment. Contentment is not achieved the same way as happiness from things like acquiring material possessions. Contentment means peace of mind.

Everything in this book serves a purpose. You've just gained insight into quotes, maxims, sources, context, metaphors, parables, and analogies to ensure you benefit significantly from what is being presented in this book.

This book is about teaching you how to think, not what to think. More specifically, it is about learning how to think for yourself. That is the most powerful tool you can possess.

Learning how to think for yourself is the greatest gift you can possess.

CHAPTER TWENTY

Acting In Leadership - The Sources

What's in a name? That which we call a rose, by any other name would smell as sweet. ~William Shakespeare, Romeo & Juliet

We compare Buddhism, Taoism, Greek Philosophy, and the *Bible* to one another as if they are different. They are a rose under different names. They all contain the attributes and blueprint for acting in leadership.

Rather than look at them through the "acting in leadership" lens, we use them as labels to separate, yet they all tell us the same things.

Sectarian labels, which are fancy ways of saying groups of people with somewhat different religious beliefs, allow us to produce harmful prejudices. A religious belief means relating to or manifesting faithful devotion to an acknowledged ultimate reality or deity. For example, since atheism can be a perceived ultimate reality, it is also a type of religion. Atheism is a religion. Therefore, when any self-proclaimed atheist belittles the concept of religion, they miss the point that they are dismissing their own belief system.

When we express our specific beliefs, we create separation. "My philosophy is the right one." "My religion is the true religion." And on and on.

In our minds, we put labels on everything. For example, when we see a person, we look at their physical features and seem to want to know if they are Chinese, European, English, American, German, Middle Eastern, African, Mexican, Brazilian, or Russian, etc.

What's odd is that children do not do this right out of the gate, yet we perpetuate this behavior as adults.

People are so fond of discriminative labels that we even go to the length of putting them on human qualities and emotions common to all of us.

The leadership lessons from the *Tao Te Ching*, *Dhammapada*, Greek philosophy, and the *Bible*, in every one of these cultures, tell us not to group and label people; we are all one under a greater power than ourselves. Then, we do just the opposite. Want a great example of irony? There you go.

Don't lie, cheat, or steal. What is the ultimate source of those behavioral guidelines? Treat others with respect, help those less fortunate, or work together for a common purpose to do good. Where did all of those life principles come from?

The attributes and the blueprint for acting in leadership have been around for thousands of years.

This similarity across cultures is the lesson Shakespeare was teaching us about life in general regarding labels. The lessons of acting in leadership come as a rose under many names.

I had not studied the history of the philosophies of Lao Tzu, Buddha, and Greek philosophers, nor had I read the *Bible* in detail before writing my first two books, nor were they part of the research.

Oh sure, I had seen quotes in other books, and in passing, perhaps on a large motivational poster inside some business I visited. Now, those quotes are scattered all over the internet. And at times, like most people, I made fun of some of the quotes. All of these early teachings, from across multiple cultures, thousands of miles apart, provide the foundational attributes for acting in leadership. Have I repeated that enough times so that it's sinking in yet?

According to the definition from Oxford Languages, there are two distinct definitions of leadership.

1) the action of leading a group of people or an organization, and
2) the state or position of being a leader.

When I looked at the two definitions of leadership, organically, I understood the first definition to be a misguided path and the second to be the natural, intended route, the enlightened road to what constitutes acting in leadership.

In the second definition, the words "state" and "position" do not infer a position in a hierarchy. Lao Tzu, Buddha, the Greek philosophers, and the *Bible* show us what "the state or position of being a leader" means.

Our beliefs and thoughts drive the actions we take or do not take. Those actions lead to a progression in either a positive or negative trajectory. Through those actions, we should be gaining insight that helps us progress in a positive trajectory by acting with integrity, remaining on the positive side of the leadership lifeline, and that will be done in collaboration with something or someone.

In chapters fifteen through eighteen, I used anger as one example of where there is alignment within Taoism, Buddhism, Greek philosophy, and biblical teachings.

Back in 450 B.C., they did not have the science about the effects of cortisol, adrenaline, dopamine, serotonin, and oxytocin we learned about in chapters eleven through thirteen. We know what chemicals anger releases. We also know that anger clouds our judgment. We do not think clearly when we are angry.

In chapter ten, we gained insight into the effects of stress and anxiety, which lead to heart disease. Just like the chemicals nature produces, we have science about stress and anxiety. All four cultures enlightened us on the causes of stress and anxiety as well as the remedies to reduce both.

Right now, you may be experiencing one of several emotions. One might be that indescribable feeling of confusion because everything you think you've been exposed to about the concept of leadership is misguided.

The most common feeling among my readers is clarity because you intrinsically understand the philosophies behind the true origins of acting in leadership but have been unable to put those thoughts into a simple, easy-to-explain, coherent structure. You can review the BASIC Leadership blueprint on the following page and apply it to the next chapter to see what the lessons of history have shown us.

Have you heard of the Manusmriti system of hierarchy?

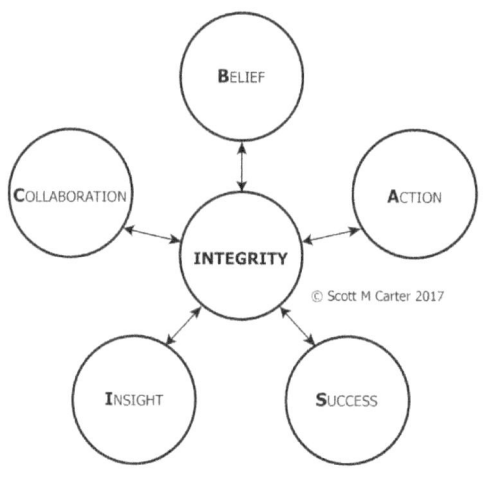

Back to BASIC™
Leadership Platform

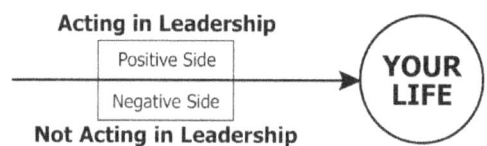

Back to BASIC™
Leadership Life Line

© Scott M Carter 2017

CHAPTER TWENTY-ONE

Divergent & Manusmriti

More Movies & Lessons

Imagine you are living three thousand years in the future when some apocalyptic event dramatically transformed planet Earth. The sky rains down a reddish sludge and most of the topsoil struggles to sustain life at any reasonable level. A toxic atmosphere requires an invisible protective shield, one large enough to cover a small city and some of the land around the city's perimeter.

In this post-apocalyptic future, everyone is divided into groups called factions. This faction system exists because a small controlling group of people decided this structure is the best way for a cohesive society to exist.

In this society, when you reach adulthood, you get to choose which faction group you want to belong to, but once that choice has been made, it is permanent. Extreme separation between the groups exist. Members of each specific faction live together, separated from the other factions. You are not allowed to visit the different factions and hang out.

If you've seen the *Divergent* movie trilogy, those vivid images pop quickly into your head. Based on novels by the American author Veronica Roth, society has been divided into factions labeled Dauntless (the brave), Amity (the kind), Erudite (the intelligent), Abnegation (the selfless), and Candor (the honest).

Each year, those who have reached the age of sixteen take a placement test that tells them their genetic behavioral category, and then they freely choose the faction to which they will devote the rest of their life.

How does this societal structure sound to you? Do you want to live in it? Do you think it would work? Which faction would you choose? If you chose Candor, could you be completely honest all the time? If others were honest with you day in and day out, could you handle it?

The Amity group farms and provides all the food for the other factions. You have to be kind to others no matter what others say or do to you. Could you do that? Once you choose Amity, you do not get to leave. You do not get to change your mind and pursue being a scientist like the Erudite, or decide to change and become part of Dauntless, the brave who provide security and do fun, exciting things like go zip lining as a reward for passing tests of courage.

Same questions. How does this societal structure sound to you? Want to live in it? Think it would work?

Which faction would you choose? What if you did not get to choose freely and you were assigned a group based on your birth associated with your lineage? Do not answer yet.

Real-Life Application

Do you believe dividing people into factions has ever been done? Has this experiment ever been played out in real life? The answer is yes. It began around 1000 B.C., peaking around 300 -100 B.C. It's called Manusmriti.

Instead of factions, the groups consist of five castes. Brahmins (priests, teachers), Kshatriyas (rulers, warriors), Vaishyas (landowners, merchants), Sudras (servants), and Dalits (untouchables).

Brahmins, Kshatriyas, Vaishyas, and Shudras, in that descending order of status and privilege, were assigned, based on birth, duties, and obligations which were fixed for life, watertight and immutable. Marriage between them was not permitted, nor could they eat together.

The Brahmins were the super-lords with exclusive privileges, and the other castes were assigned duties necessary for their protection and preservation. The Kshatriyas were to protect and defend the land, the Vaishyas were to produce food by tilling the land and tending the animals and plants, and also to trade in the produce, and the Shudras were the bottom of the hierarchy, lacking any skill or semblance of prestige. Want to know how it worked out? Not well.

You see, these kinds of things almost always come into existence because of the pursuit of power and hierarchical authority, seeking to rein over others. They eventually fail. People naturally push back against control and authority of this type because it is in direct contrast to the principles behind acting in leadership.

Pushback against the Manusmriti drove an extreme rise in the followers of what we know today as Buddhism. Why? Because, Buddhism teaches acting in leadership, and acting in leadership does not require a person to be in a high-level position in any hierarchical system.

In 2023, in the United States, and globally, we see people exhibiting the behaviors of the old Manusmriti, most of which are playing out in the political world. These types of behaviors have always existed within societies, and sadly, they will always exist.

Some would see us put into castes or factions and assigned our jobs so they could rule and live well. They are like the Dalits and Brahmins, few in number, yet have established themselves in positions of hierarchical authority, and they wish to rule over all of us. And we call them leaders. That's a real eye-opener isn't it?

Politicians, and the big business moguls they are in bed with, they believe leadership is a position in a hierarchy, and that they must have followers, either voluntarily or by force, to attain the title of leader. They work heavily to influence us through marketing (propaganda).

In chapter thirty-two of the Tao Te Ching, the "it" in the first line refers to "the way," which is acting in leadership.

If princes and kings could follow it,
all things would by themselves abide,
Heaven and Earth would unite
and sweet dew would fall.
People would by themselves find harmony,
without being commanded.
    ~Lao Tzu, *Tao Te Ching*[1]

Chapter twenty-six of the Dhammapada defines the true Brahmin. Remember, in the Manusmriti system, the Brahmins were the super-lords with exclusive privileges, and the other castes were assigned duties necessary for their protection and preservation. Buddhism is one of the early arguments against leadership being attached to a position in a hierarchy. Here is stanza from chapter twenty-six.

That one I call a brahmin who is never angry,
never causes harm to others even when harmed
by them.
    ~Buddha, *The Dhammapada*[2]

Those actions and traits mirror the actions and traits we say leaders should exhibit in the twenty-first century. The difference is that we are still attaching them to the top positions in a hierarchy, which drives us back toward the Manusmriti system. Scary huh?

The philosophies of four distinct cultures, thousands of miles apart, all enlighten us on the fact that if society can govern itself, live in reasonable harmony, and everyone takes personal responsibility for their own actions, acting with integrity, on the positive side of the lifeline, then those who seek power become obsolete, unnecessary.

This does not mean that the existence of any hierarchy that creates a cohesiveness in a society should be eliminated; it means that those who seek to rule for power, aka those who do not act in leadership, should not be in those upper hierarchical positions.

The following passage from the Tao Te Ching is part of a larger context illustrating how, within a society, when all people act in leadership, no action is required from others within the hierarchy.

> *Therefore the sage says:*
> *I do not act,*
> *And the people become reformed by themselves.*
> *I am at peace,*
> *And the people become fair by themselves.*
> *I do not interfere,*
> *And the people become rich by themselves.*
> *I have no desire to desire,*
> *And the people become like uncarved wood by themselves.*
> ~Lao Tzu, Tao Te Ching[3]

We can easily see how the Tao Te Ching and the Dhammapada teach the same societal principle. The following verse is part of a larger context about how everyone is responsible for acting in leadership. It also includes verses about how a person at the top of the hierarchy should only be there if they act in leadership.

> *Your own self is your master; who else could be?*
> *With yourself well controlled, you gain mastery very*
> *hard to find.*
>
> *Learn what is right; then teach others, as*
> *the wise do. Before trying to guide others, be your*
> *own guide first. It is hard to learn to guide oneself.*
> ~Buddha, The Dhammapada[4]

In the *Bible*, this same lesson exists in Genesis. The overall context in Genesis 2:4-25 tells us that from the beginning, each individual counts and is accountable and that ideas and actions have consequences. Adam and Eve were lousy self-governors, and there were consequences. Genesis illustrates how we have free will; along with that, we can experience self-inflicted shame and guilt by not acting in leadership.

The 147 Greek maxims contain abundance guidance on how it all begins with self-governing. If everyone in a society acts in leadership according to this guidance, very little governing is needed.

- *Control Yourself*
- *Control Anger*
- *Cling to discipline*
- *Practice what is just*
- *Exercise nobility of character*
- *Shun Evil*

All of the guidance within these vastly separated cultures directly opposes the Manusmriti system. Manusmriti systems cause conflict and disunity.

Today's castes and factions are based on race, ethnicity, religion, and other labels. In basic terms, race describes physical traits, and ethnicity refers to cultural identification—Black, White, Hispanic, Asian, African, Indian of Middle Eastern descent, Christian, atheist, Buddhist, and so on.

Some want to divide society into various social groups, then create the appearance of conflicting interests, antagonistic to each other, distrust builds, and then a social construct as the solution is offered up by those wishing to rule. Then, under the first definition of leadership, we give those who rule the label of leader. See how easy this is to understand?

The Manusmriti system, over time, created an extensive number of sub-castes, all birth-based, socially isolated from one another, and unfriendly and hostile to each other. This hierarchical system ensures those on the lowest levels would always remain there. Anything that creates intolerance, mistrust, and disunity stems from a dystopian mindset, the opposite of a society that acting in leadership would produce.

In the *Divergent* movie series, the main character, Trish, was a perfect balance of all five attributes of all five factions and, therefore, deemed a threat to society because she could not be classified and controlled.

In 2024, when this book will be published, anyone who thinks for themselves, anyone who takes responsibility for their own actions, and anyone who does not to look to a societal government to solve all their problems is fast becoming labeled as a threat to society by many who wish to rule in the political classes. In other words, anyone who acts in leadership under the BASIC Leadership blueprint.

Acting in leadership, in its true essence, is the opposite of any Manusmriti-type system. This is why people who gain insight into the teachings of Taoism, Buddhism, Greek philosophy, and the lessons of the *Bible* are naturally drawn to learn more, and most desire for society to act in accordance with these teachings.

Yes, hierarchies are necessary and beneficial to a degree. These teachings, the philosophies behind the true essence of acting in leadership, threaten hierarchical structures where the intent of those at the top is to rule over others using tactics that land on the negative side of the leadership lifeline.

The goal is to progress toward living in leadership and acting in leadership, as often as possible. Anyone, regardless of their personality profile is capable of acting in leadership.

CHAPTER TWENTY-TWO

Time, Effort, Trade-Offs, and Guarantees

We are all more alike in so many ways than we are different. We can see this in our general physical appearance: legs, arms, head, ears, eyes, mouth, etc.

Not exactly the same, but did you know that according to the National Human Genome Research Institute, HIH, All human beings are 99.9% identical in their genetic makeup? We are also 99.9% the same when it comes to time, effort, and trade-offs.

Time

How many hours in a day do you have? The answer is identical for everyone: 24 hours. That's 1,440 minutes. We get to decide how we utilize that time. One primary reason our lives are different is based on where and how we spend that time.

Time is the movement of the sun, a measure of its motion. ~Plato

We do not need more quotes about time. That one sums it all up. Time is an invention. Where and how we spend our time matters because time is our most precious personal resource. One day, your time will run out, and in the end, you will contemplate where and how you spent it.

Effort

It takes effort to do everything, even to do nothing. We say things like, "Work smarter, not harder." We end up trying to create solutions to the very problems we create ourselves. You create most of the stress and anxiety in your life. You spend time and effort doing that, then spend more time and effort trying to counteract it. Does that sound like you're working smarter, not harder?

Act without doing;
work without effort.
Think of the small as large
and the few as many.
Confront the difficult
while it is still easy;
accomplish the great task
by a series of small acts.
The Master never reaches for great;
Thus she achieves greatness.
   ~Lao Tzu, *Tao Te Ching*[1]

Chapter 63 of the *Tao Te Ching* combines multiple insights about effort. Act without doing alludes to not forcing things. The Tao tells us not to force things, not to escalate.

Wake up! Don't be lazy. Follow the
right path, avoid the wrong. You will be
happy here as well as hereafter.
~Buddha, *The Dhammapada*[2]

In the *Dhammapada*, it says outright not to be lazy. It also illustrates how making a "natural" effort is where contentment comes from in life. Make an effort you know to be true to your full potential, and you will have peace of mind that you did so then yesterday becomes a thing of the past with no anxiety about whether you did your best and acted rightly. It puts your focus on *today*, not the future.

The end aimed at is not knowledge but action.
~Aristotle[3]

Aristotle tells us that knowledge without action is useless. We saw an earlier quote from Al-Ghazâlî.

Knowledge without action is wastefulness, and action
without knowledge is foolish. ~Al-Ghazâlî

Pray to the gods only when you're making some effort
on your own behalf; otherwise your prayers are
wasted! ~Aesop, Heracles and the Driver

Ever wonder where the English proverb "God helps them who help themselves" comes from? There you go. It was Aesop, a slave boy who lived roughly 70 years before Socrates. The number of Greek quotes about effort, action, and the lessons they teach could be an entire chapter itself.

The Bible tells us we must make an effort, do so with integrity, and focus on the positive side of the leadership lifeline. This lesson comes from the Old Testament, 3,500 years ago.

> *The Lord will send a blessing on your barns and on everything you put your hand to. The Lord your God will bless you in the land he is giving you.*
> ~Deuteronomy 28:8 (NIV)

People do not want to put in the effort but expect things to happen. "Put your hand to," means plain old hard work. People think the phrase "work smarter, not harder" means they'll never have to put on a pair of jeans and get their hands dirty. Let someone else do it. I'll just bark out orders or oversee others putting in the effort. That makes me a leader. *Wrong!*

We're talking about a controlled, intentional effort, one that is natural in its progression. In the next chapter, we'll see what this means when we define the difference between a natural progression and an escalation.

Trade-Offs

I ended the time component of this chapter with, "It's where and how we spend our time that matters." I knew where most people's minds went when reacting to the first two components: time and effort.

"Too many things on your plate. Not enough time. So much to do and so little time to. do it all." So little time?

It's the same for everyone; 1,440 minutes hasn't changed since you read that number just a few paragraphs ago. It's not that you have so little time; your issue is that you have not decided what to include or *not* include in your days and life. If you want to reduce stress and anxiety, then you must decide what to trade-off.

> *Trade-offs have been with us ever since the late unpleasantness in the Garden of Eden.* ~Thomas Sowell

Thomas Sowell also said, "There are no solutions; there are only trade-offs." He is correct, but not because solutions do not exist. Solutions are never permanent; they are a continuing progression. The five BASIC outer ring components show this to be true.

> *All solutions require trade-offs. Solutions are never permanent; they are ongoing progressions with never-ending trade-offs.* ~Scott M. Carter

In the movie *Avengers: Infinity War*, Thanos sacrifices his daughter Gamora to get the soul stone. When Thanos and Gamora see the large cliff and what appears to be a place of sacrifice, Gamora asks the stone keeper, "What's this?" The keeper replies, "The price. The stone holds a special place among the infinity stones. You might say it has a certain wisdom."

This scene is one of the best analogies about selling our souls for power. There is always a trade-off. The language often used today is "a price to pay" or "everything comes at a cost." The price is often high when a person does not act in leadership. Thanos must sacrifice his daughter Gamora to get the soul stone. In the next movie in the series, *Avengers: End Game*, when asked what acquiring the infinity stones cost him, Thanos replies, "Everything." Getting the soul stone cost him his soul.

> It is unreasonable to think we can earn rewards without being willing to pay their true price. It is always our choice whether or not we wish to pay the price for life's rewards. ~Epictetus, *The Enchiridion*

Epictetus was a stoic philosopher who lived at the same time as Jesus.

> Evildoers may be happy as long as they do
> not reap what they have sown, but when they
> do sorrow overcomes them. The good may
> suffer as long as they do not reap what they have
> sown, but when they do, joy overcomes them.
>   ~Buddha, The Dhammapada[4]

In this verse, Buddha tells us that there is no guarantee of punishment when a person does not act rightly. We then use that as an excuse not to act rightly ourselves. Buddha also tells us that there is no guarantee that we will get some sort of reward for acting rightly. So, we use that as an excuse not to act rightly.

We make excuses like, "Bob cheated, and nothing bad happened to him," or "I saw this old guy who is 90, and he smoked all his life," or "Sally has incredible integrity and acts in leadership most of the time, and she's not wealthy." Those are excuses not to act in leadership. No one anywhere, ever, told us there were guarantees associated with acting in leadership. We confuse trade-offs with guarantees.

There is always a trade-off for everything, but there is no guarantee of punishment or reward for acting or not acting in leadership.

Sit on your tushy a lot and eat unhealthy foods; what is the result? Obesity and an unhealthy body. Then we see a skinny person who eats anything and doesn't get fat, so we make up excuses not to do what we need to do. It doesn't mean that person isn't damaging their physical being just because we can't see it.

Obesity and an unhealthy body are potential trade-offs. The crappy food is yummy. We all know it. Pick your tasty treat. Cookies, ice cream, sodas, potato chips, cake. Is your mouth salivating yet? A massive plate of lasagna, a fully loaded supreme pizza, or a huge pile of mashed potatoes and stuffing smothered in gravy.

Let's not forget that frothy, caramel, or chocolatey caffeinated drink you absolutely cannot live without to get your day started. How about a burger and fries, and lets supersize it? Ready to head to the kitchen or yank your steering wheel into the nearest drive-thru window?

Some trade-offs for unhealthy eating decisions are obesity, being tired all the time, and even early death. There's a long list of things that fall on the negative side of the Leadership Lifeline. All of it is based on your beliefs, followed by your actions. Then progressing toward something, and collaborating with others or other things.

You will blame it on addiction or some other disorder the propagandists tell you, so they sell you their product, service, and, worst of all, a pile of drugs from pharmaceutical companies. "Go ahead, get fat; we're making a pill for that." Sounds like lyrics from a rap song.

Then, you can experience all the side effects of that drug. In either case, when you blame someone else for all of it, the blame of this kind falls on the negative side of the leadership lifeline.

It reminds me of the scene in the movie *Shrek 2* where Shrek, Donkey, and Puss In Boots have stolen a magical potion from the Fairy Godmother. Puss In Poots sees a label on the bottle and reads it.

> *Happily Ever After Potion. Maximum strength. For you and your true love. If one of you drinks this, you will both be fine, happiness, comfort and beauty divine. Fair relief of symptoms due to common unhappiness.*
>
> *WARNING: side effects may include burning, itching, oozing, weeping. Not intended for heart patients or those with nervous disorders. To make the effects of the potion permanent the drinker must obtain his or her true love's first kiss by midnight.*

The writers are making fun of all the commercials we are exposed to on TV, radio, the internet, pop-up ads, etc. Propaganda under the label of marketing. That's adult humor in a kid's movie, and it's also a depiction of reality. There will always be trade-offs. We make fun of things when we can relate them to real life. Of course,

Shrek drinks it, then farts because toot jokes make us laugh. Here, pull my finger.

When you have gained insight into what makes you healthy, and knowledge of what makes you unhealthy, and you fail to act on it by following the worthy ideal of progressively becoming healthier, then you have failed to act in leadership.

We always progress toward something. The outer wheel of the BASIC Leadership platform is how life works in general. The integrity hub and leadership lifeline help us define acting in leadership. See how easy the BASIC blueprint is for determining when a person acts in leadership? Is this stuff easy, or what?

Remember, in chapter fourteen, Elon Musk taught us to use Semantic Tree Learning and to start with an intuitive understanding of the basics, the foundational principles.

The seven components of the BASIC Leadership blueprint make up the trunk of the oak tree, the foundation. Once we understand that, then we can take any small detail, like the leaves of the tree, and see how it either defines acting in leadership or not acting in leadership.

There's always a trade-off. If you want to act in leadership by eating healthy, you must give up what makes you unhealthy. You might even have to change the people you associate with because they influence you not to act in leadership. Are you prepared to make that trade-off? Alcoholics Anonymous applies this principle to help people who struggle with addiction.

No matter which path you take, acting in leadership or not acting in leadership, you put in time and effort. It takes time and effort to shop for crappy food and healthy food. It takes time and effort to eat healthy and unhealthy food.

"I don't have time to eat healthy" is a load of poop. "I can't afford to eat healthy" is a load of crap. Based solely on misguided beliefs, leading to poor decisions, which leads to actions that fall on the negative side of the leadership lifeline. Anything unethical about eating junk foods? Perhaps a lack of integrity? I say, "Yes." Let me prove it to you.

People whine about the cost of healthcare, yet they do not eat healthily or exercise. Unhealthy eating and lack of exercise leads to poor health in large numbers within a prospering society, which overtaxes the healthcare systems. All of this can be avoided. Once you have this information, meaning you've gained insight into it, and you do not act accordingly, could we then consider that a lack of integrity?

Integrity is the quality of being honest and having strong moral principles; moral uprightness. Based on the definition of integrity, the answer is an absolute "yes."

By default, any person who knows that eating unhealthily and not exercising puts a burden on society and does not act accordingly lacks integrity. That's what the leadership lifeline does for us. It helps us tie things into the integrity hub. The only exercise some people get is jumping to conclusions, running off at the mouth, pulling others down to their level, digging up dirt, and dodging responsibility.

The good news is that all of these early philosophies also tell us, "all things in moderation." Live healthy most of the time, and you can enjoy a dessert or two in moderation. Now, you can stop the self-inflicted suffering of guilt when eating a cookie or self-inflicted anxiety because you think you cannot enjoy the occasional dessert.

I eat sweets and desserts; when I do, I do not feel guilty because I do it in moderation. The little black dot in the larger white portion of the yin-yang symbol also represent moderation. Life is a balance.

Again, this is not a health book or a finance book; this is a book that defines what it means to act in leadership, and I am arguing my case for how the BASIC Leadership blueprint does exactly that, and it does so in alignment with the principles and lessons known for thousands of years.

BASIC™ Leadership Guarantees

> *Whether you think you can, or you think you can't –* *you're right.* ~Henry Ford

We learned that there is no guarantee of punishment or reward for acting in or not acting in leadership. I can, however, make you the following guarantees.

✓ Your beliefs will cause you to act or not to act.

✓ You will always be progressing in a trajectory in your life. Life moves forward.

✓ You have more control than you think you do regarding that trajectory.

✓ Your life will contain adversity, difficulty, and challenges. They exist for everyone.

✓ Acting in leadership best prepares you for those adversities, difficulties, and challenges.

✓ You can achieve your highest level of contentment and peace of mind only through acting in leadership.

These things will become self-evident as you continue to gain insight throughout this book.

A statement is persuasive and credible either because it is directly self-evident or because it appears to be proved from other statements that are so. ~Aristotle[5]

Next, let's gain some insight. What's the difference between a progression versus an escalation?

CHAPTER TWENTY-THREE

Progression or Escalation?

In chapter ten, we began our journey of gaining insight into the effects of stress and anxiety. Dr. Elliot and his team created the Institute of Stress Medicine in Denver, Colorado. Stress and anxiety, known as the silent killers, land on the negative side of the leadership lifeline.

One of the five components of the BASIC Leadership outer ring is Success, which is the progressive realization of a worthy ideal. If I asked you the difference between progression and escalation, could you explain it in simple terms?

To understand what acting in leadership means, we must understand the difference between a progression and an escalation. Escalation is one of the causes of many things we know that leaders are supposed to avoid. Yet most leadership platforms promote escalation as success.

I lost count of the number of books with interviews containing "I was raised in a high-expectation, high-performance household," or similar phrases that depict how people live a life of escalation. They misguidedly call it success. It's like saying that success in life is driving really fast every day in a high-performance race car. Let's all do that daily on the freeway and see how it turns out.

The difference between progression and escalation can be significant

> Progression: *the process of developing or moving gradually towards a more advanced state.*

> Escalation: *an increase in the intensity or seriousness of something; an intensification*

Which one do you think causes mental tensions such as stress, anxiety, fear, worry, nervousness, and uncertainty? You are correct; it's escalation. Which one do you think the early philosophers warned us about? You are correct again; it's escalation. Is leadership about creating stress, anxiety, fear, worry, or uncertainly?

Like many concepts. the difference between progression and escalation might appear cloudy and subjective. However, as we are quickly learning, the methods for helping us achieve clarity have been around for thousands of years. Aristotle developed a schematic of virtues and their extremes.

Too Little	Balance	Too Much
sloth	ambition	greed
cowardice	courage	rashness
humility	modesty	pride

The three columns are like the lesson taught in the fable *Goldie Locks and the Three Bears*, except for the breaking in and entering part. The papa bear's porridge was too hot, the momma bear's porridge was too cold, and the baby bear's porridge was just right.

Aristotle put together this table of virtues to address fear and confidence, pleasure and pain, earning and spending, honor and dishonor, anger, shame, and social conduct. It's an extensive list.

We can escalate in both directions: too much and too little. Extreme laziness, sloth, is a form of escalation on the negative side of the leadership lifeline.

We can also confuse progression with a never-ending increase. Our age is a naturally increasing progression, but staying healthy does not work the same way. Staying healthy as we age requires a progression of changes in how we remain healthy, in turn, allowing us to retain our optimal health. As we age, our bodies will change, and we cannot continue to do the things we used to do physically. Progression does not imply or require any sort of numerical or statistical increase.

Buddha enlightened us with the four noble truths. The second truth, known as Samudaya, provides the origin of these sufferings related to separation from the pleasant and not gaining what we desire based on cravings and attachment in a never-ending cycle of escalation.

Lao Tzu enlightened us about the effects of simplicity, patience, and letting go, the opposite of escalation. The *Bible* also covered these same concepts.

None of these early teachings of acting in leadership say, "not to do anything." They provide guidance on how to progress in life. They tell us to act like nature. They use nature as a metaphor. Remember, metaphors help us convert abstract concepts into concrete images so we can understand them.

When you stare at nature, can you see the grass, trees, flowers, or other things growing? No, yet they do so little by little. That's a natural progression. We've been propagandized to escalate everything in our lives.

Do you believe that a life with little or no stress, anxiety, fear, worry, and uncertainty is a good thing? Most people do. We're told that leaders remain calm and focus on courage, not fear.

> *Truly, only those who see illness as illness*
> *Can avoid illness.*
> *The sage is not ill,*
> *Because he sees illness as illness.*
> *Therefore he is not ill.*
> ~Lao Tzu, *Tao Te Ching*[1]

Lao Tzu is not talking about influenza or the common cold. When a person recognizes stress, anxiety, fear, worry, and uncertainty as illnesses and then acts to rectify the root causes, that person will no longer be ill.

They will not do the self-inflicted actions that cause the suffering brought on by stress, anxiety, fear, uncertainty, and worry. We know the root causes of most stress in our lives. Most of it is escalation. We also see how too little, which is a diminishing of ourselves, can cause stress, anxiety, and depression.

Right now, society is focused on the massive rise in escalation derived from the industrialization of societies.

Ethical Fading, Propaganda, and Influence

In 1975, British economist Charles Goodhart jokingly stated that "Any observed statistical regularity will tend to collapse once pressure is placed upon it for control purposes." That turned into Goodhart's Law.

> *When a measure becomes a target,*
> *it ceases to be a good measure.*
> ~Goodhart's Law

When we set a specific goal, people will tend to optimize for that objective regardless of the consequences. The minute a person begins to cut corners and violate principles and ethics, aka integrity, something called ethical fading occurs.

Ethical fading happens when we take an arbitrary goal and incentivize it with a carrot, a reward. The person desires the carrot, so they cut corners somewhere to meet the assigned number. We start by cutting small ethical corners; this becomes the norm, and then we learn how to cut bigger ones.

I discussed this in more detail in my first book, *Leadership: Achieving Optimal Effectiveness.* The point is that whenever we escalate, it leads to violating the integrity hub and our ability to land on the positive side of the leadership lifeline. The concept of ethical fading has always existed, but its deep roots took hold in business during the large industrialization of the United States and have now filtered into every part of our daily lives.

In 1976, Stuart Ewen published *Captains of Consciousness,* updated in 2001. The premise? He studied marketing (propaganda) during the early large-scale industrialization of the United States.

He outlines the history and methods of marketing, showing us how people have been trained to desire mass-produced goods that, just a few years before, they didn't know they wanted. Think about that statement for a minute: *trained to desire mass-produced goods that, just a few years before, they didn't know they wanted.* Yikes!

In chapter nine, we learned about Edward Bernays's book Propaganda. Bernays provided us with insight in 1928, and Stuart Ewan again in 1976. From 1928 to 1976, businesses became even more proficient at propaganda under the name marketing. Imagine how much more proficient they might be at manipulating society to not act in leadership by the time you are reading this book.

In 1984, the book *Influence: The Psychology of Persuasion* was published. Written by Robert Cialdini,

Ph. D., it enlightens us on six principles of influence: reciprocation, commitment and consistency, social proof, liking, authority, and scarcity.

Then, in 2016, his book *Pre-Suasion: A Revolutionary Way to Influence and Persuade* was published. In business, we can learn how to "presuade" before we "persuade." These tools are being used on us every single day by businesses. I've seen Cialdini speak in person. His books provide incredible insight. If you have a marketing degree, you could have skipped the four years of college and read the four books I have mentioned above. You'd be way ahead of the game in business.

We have been heavily influenced to compare ourselves to others and to align who and what we are with material things. You've been told you need to be special in order to be loved. You've been told that leadership is about being "extraordinary." You've been told that leaders and leadership exist at the top of hierarchies, creating an atmosphere of competition to become a leader. What a disservice to the concept of acting in leadership.

The following verses of the Dhammapada tell us that our innate desires and compulsions cause us to go beyond meeting our natural needs, creating self-inflicted suffering. Escalation cannot, and never will, fill any void to achieve peace and contentment.

*The compulsive urges of the thoughtless grow
like a creeper. They jump like a monkey from one*

life to another, looking for fruit in the forest.

When these urges drive us, sorrow spreads
like wild grass. Conquer these fierce
cravings and sorrow will fall away from your
life like drops of water from a lotus leaf.
    ~Buddha, *The Dhammapada*[2]

Attempting to gain 15% in growth for the sake of stockholders is escalation. Attempts to achieve that goal, and not achieving it, cause suffering. Heads up, achieving it also does. Achieving it leads you to believe all the previous stress and anxiety was worth it, so you do more of it. This is a vicious and damaging cycle in contrast to acting in leadership in its true essence.

This means that when a corporation sets and drives toward such a goal, it does not constitute acting in leadership, as some might believe. It is escalation and is a root cause of anxiety, stress, fear, and many other elements that exist on the negative side of the leadership lifeline. It is also a primary factor leading to ethical fading.

The idea of stock-held companies is an invention. Many inventions drive escalation. Go ahead, set that goal, and drive toward it. I do not care. Just stop calling that a form of leadership. You're the CEO of a corporation driving the business objective of 15% growth to meet the expectations of stockholders and investors. You are not a leader because of your position in a hierarchy where your responsibility is driving a random, mandated increase in stock value. Let's call it what it is, which is doing business.

Similarly, setting a goal of making a million dollars by age XX is a form of escalation. Who told you that a college degree is a necessity? I'd hire a person without a college degree who has read the four books I previously mentioned before I'd hire a person with a four-year degree who hasn't read them.

Sure, we want doctors to be well educated, and we certainly want an engineer who builds bridges to know what the heck he or she is doing, but higher education is a business, no different than producing clothing. In my first book, I provided a list of people who did incredible things without any higher education as we know it today.

Please do not confuse what I am saying here with telling you what you can or cannot do. That is not my place nor the focus of this book. Did you need to win before someone told you it was about winning? Before you see an ad for some product or service, did you ever think about that product or service? Did you actually need it? The answer is no. Start thinking for yourself.

You now have a deficiency you didn't know you had. You now have a disease or symptom you didn't have five minutes ago. We are taught what we need and want, then shown products and services that will theoretically satisfy those wants and needs. All of it drives an escalation, not a progression. In short, marketing techniques generate and channel desire. Why do these tactics work? They are based on fear, lust, shame, and greed, to name a few, which are all things that land on the negative side of the leadership lifeline. It also includes everything that aligns with the "too little and too much" categories in Aristotle's extreme virtues table.

In chapter twenty-one, we learned how political tactics influence us to pit ourselves against one another, mirroring the Manusmriti system of hierarchies. These kinds of tactics, including escalation, are everywhere. As a society, we self-inflict stress, anxiety, fear, worry, nervousness, and uncertainty upon ourselves through many things, including escalation. It is not new. It's been known for thousands of years.

The reason we have so much stress, anxiety, fear, worry, and uncertainty in our lives and the world?

1) We are not taught how to deal with those things from an early age through the lessons of acting in leadership.
2) We are taught to escalate everything in our lives, which increases the very things acting in leadership teaches us how to reduce or avoid.

The solution? Stop escalating. We're escalating and attempting to treat the symptoms rather than address the root cause. We create misguided leadership labels such as transactional leadership, situational leadership, or transformational leadership. There are hundreds of these misguided labels that treat the symptoms of people not acting in leadership.

CHAPTER TWENTY-FOUR

Root Cause or Symptom?

A symptom happens as a result of the root cause of a problem. The Flu is a contagious respiratory illness caused by influenza viruses that infect the nose, throat, and sometimes the lungs. The root cause is the influenza virus. We treat the symptoms, including headaches, runny noses, coughs, and fevers, with a multitude of medications.

We live in a world where the standard has become treating symptoms rather than addressing the root cause. The BASIC Leadership blueprint addresses the root causes of people's failure to act in leadership. Most of what we hear and read about leadership addresses the symptoms.

We know that according to the Centers for Disease Control, the CDC, heart disease is the leading cause of death in the United States. Unhealthy diet, physical inactivity, and stress are three of the root causes. Of those three, stress is called the silent killer.

In chapter ten, we learned about Dr. Eliot, the Chief of Cardiology at the University of Nebraska, who went on to help create the Institute of Stress Medicine in Denver, Colorado.

The Institute of Stress Medicine in Denver, Colorado had been around for over 40 years when I wrote this book. Most people, and by most, I mean at least 99.9% of the people who read this book, have never heard of Dr. Eliot or the Stress Institute. Probably not many more, but a few more might be familiar with the food pyramid.

What do you suppose you might find if you research the food pyramid and its history? There are several versions. The 1974 version from Sweden looks like the image below. Starting from the first layer on the bottom, you eat a larger amount of those items and less of each as you move upward on the pyramid.

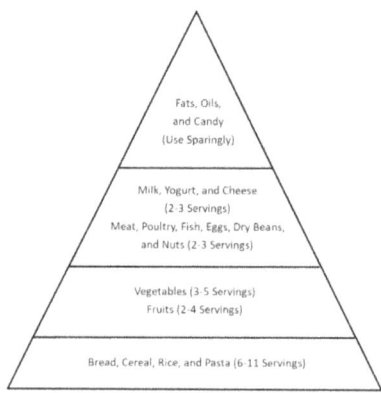

First Layer: Breads, Cereals, Potatoes, Rice, Pasta
            (6 – 11 servings)
Second Layer: Vegetables (3 – 5 servings)
            Fruits (2 – 4 servings)
Third Layer: Yogurt, Milk and Cheese (2 – 3 servings)
            Meat, Poultry, Fish, Eggs, Dry Beans, Nuts
            (2 – 3 servings)
Fifth Layer: Fats, Oils, and Candy (eat sparingly)

Here is my question: Do you think the food pyramid is based on science that is related to helping you achieve optimal health? The answer is a stern *No!*

Scientists or M.D.s did not produce the food pyramid, although some consulted because they were well-known, almost celebrity-like. The food pyramid was created in the 1970s in Sweden, and then adopted by the U.S. Department of Agriculture (USDA) in 1992.

If the food pyramid was not created by scientists for optimal health, why does it exist? It was designed to deal with food shortages—yep, food shortages. They needed something that would allow a society to produce lots of food while meeting four criteria.

1) It needed to be scalable
2) It could not cost too much
3) It has to be non-perishable and portable
4) It has to taste good (at least not yucky)

This concept began well before Sweden developed their pyramid. In 1943, the USDA released the Basic Seven Food Guide to help citizens cope with food rationing during World War II. Then, in the 1970s, the National Board of Health and Welfare was tasked with tackling rising food costs in Sweden

If you have ever been in a brainstorming meeting to solve any issue, that list of four criteria used to create the food pyramid makes perfect sense. It needed to be scalable; It could not cost too much. It has to be non-perishable and portable. It has to taste good, or at least not like a poop sandwich.

Some people gathered together and said, "This is our issue." They then produced a list of criteria that would need to be met to reach an optimal level of effectiveness.

The goal was not "to make people healthy." It was to be able to produce a large amount of food, irrespective of its nutritional or health value, do it cheaply, make sure it won't quickly rot or go bad, and it couldn't make people go "yuk, ack, patootie." Otherwise, things that taste like kale would have been the solution. Take a bite of kale and tell others it's yummy. That's not going to happen.

The food pyramid addressed the root causes of food shortages and rising food costs, but did not address the root causes of unhealthy eating. What is the result of addressing the root causes of food shortages? Lots of carbohydrates—not just carbohydrates, but processed carbohydrates.

Carbohydrates contain lots of calories, and they are inexpensive. Processed carbohydrates solve the issue of starvation and lack of calories. They can be cheaply produced so that they have a long shelf life, they are easy to transport, and a person can make them taste good if bland and starchy is your idea of "tastes good."

Those same processes that keep that food from going bad also strip out natural nutrients, which need to be artificially replaced by nutrients that our bodies do not effectively absorb. For example, processing milk removes the fats, and then we fortify the milk with vitamins A and D. The issue is that fat is required to absorb those two vitamins. And we haven't even mentioned the preservatives and other additives used. How are we doing so far?

What we have today is the solution that meets those four criteria: scalable, low cost, non-perishable, and acceptable tasting. "Here's our problem. This is the solution." The solution to the problem is what created the Standard American Diet, the SAD, the food pyramid. The acronym SAD kind of says it all, doesn't it?

The food pyramid is not a healthy eating plan. That was not its objective. It wasn't produced by scientists or M.D.s. Then, why do we still follow it? We're being misled about what eating habits address the root causes of being unhealthy. The food pyramid does not address getting healthier; eating healthy does. They are two distinctly different things with some content that crosses over between the two.

The misguided beliefs about the food pyramid mirror my argument about what constitutes acting in leadership in its true essence. Let's review the definitions of leadership from the Oxford Languages Dictionary.

1) the action of leading a group of people or an organization, and
2) the state or position of being a leader.

Most modern-day leadership solutions address the symptoms of people who do not act in leadership because they attach leadership to a position in a hierarchy.

The BASIC Leadership blueprint addresses the root causes because it is based on the second definition. My goal in defining what it means to act in leadership needed to address the root causes of not acting in leadership, then present the blueprint for acting in leadership.

Acting in leadership addresses the root causes of things, not the treatment of the symptoms. Remember, in chapter ten, I told you that we're being fed a lot of crap, and it's slowly killing us. That crap includes terrible advice on what foods to eat and propaganda about what it means to act in leadership.

We do not act in leadership by eating healthily and exercising, which addresses some of the root causes of being unhealthy. Then, after the damage is done, we want to treat the symptoms of obesity through medication, surgery, or other methods.

By examining how we have approached nutrition, we can begin to understand how to approach the concept of leadership. That is how I ended up with the BASIC Leadership blueprint. I wanted to address the root causes of people not acting in leadership.

Just like the food pyramid is a solution for coping with food shortages, most of what is being presented as leadership are solutions to business problems. The first definition of leadership shown on the previous page attaches leadership to a position in a hierarchy; the second one is represented by the BASIC Leadership blueprint, which I present in this book.

We Must Change

If we keep following the advice of the food pyramid, which is designed to address hunger and rationing issues, will society as a whole become healthier? The answer is no. We must change. Yes, there is still hunger and absolute poverty in the world. If we choose to do so, we can reduce that hunger by following the four criteria of a food supply that needs to be scalable, not cost too much, be non-perishable and portable, and taste somewhat good. Then, provide food to those in need globally, or better yet, help those societies grow food in large quantities. A good question is, why haven't we done that yet? But that discussion will have to be in another book.

Continuing to use the food pyramid under misguided beliefs about nutrition is absurd. The same can be said for leadership. It is also absurd to continue operating under the many misguided leadership labels that address the symptoms of poorly operated businesses.

Operating under the premise that one must have followers to be considered a leader has everyone out searching for followers, which has nothing to do with acting in leadership. This false leader-follower premise has been understood for a long time. In his book, *The Peter Principle* (1969), Dr. Laurence J. Peter tells us that the premise of a person having to be a good follower in order to be a good leader is one of many hierarchy fallacies circulating around. The leader-follower premise is a misguided myth.

Similarly, the premise that leadership is about influence has people running around influencing people and has nothing to do with people acting in leadership.

I do not doubt that you, like most other people, leaned back to pause for a minute and ask these questions.

- ✓ Do the current definitions of leadership address symptoms or root causes?
- ✓ Do the current definitions of leadership address the issues associated with hierarchical challenges of doing business, rather than the root causes of people, as a whole, not acting in leadership?

Next, you and I will take a closer look at the positive and negative attributes associated with the leadership lifeline. After gaining some more insight, you tell me if most of today's leadership definitions have anything to do with acting in leadership or are they designed to treat the symptoms of issues associated with doing business and escalation. Acting in leadership and doing business are distinctly different.

CHAPTER TWENTY-FIVE

Positive or Negative?

In chapter eight we learned about the seventh component of the BASIC Leadership blueprint, the Leadership Lifeline.

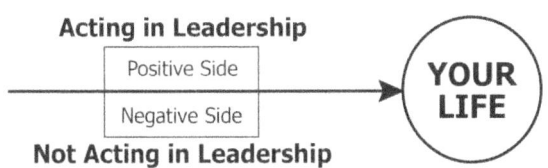

Back to BASIC™
Leadership Life Line

© Scott M Carter 2017

The integrity hub and the leadership lifeline allow us to determine when a person is acting in leadership, at least for most things. As a person progresses toward a worthy ideal, they will continually evaluate everything against the integrity hub and leadership lifeline.

The 147 maxims within the temple of Apollo contained beliefs such as "Rule your wife." Today, we know this to be bad advice. Sometimes, people get things wrong, but more often than not, we are simply ignorant. Ignorance is the lack of knowledge. It does not mean a person is stupid. The need for an intuitive understanding is critical, and also why the component of insight is so powerful. Insight; the capacity to gain an accurate and intuitive understanding.

Not all things can be measured or determined as positive or negative. For example, top & bottom, dark & light, or right & left. There is no positive or negative associated with those contrasting terms. You can't have the concept of long without the concept of short. These types of things are just a way of communicating. However, we can measure most things in terms of positive or negative when it comes to acting in leadership.

If I asked you which side of the leadership lifeline lust, gluttony, greed, sloth, wrath, envy, and pride exist, the answer is easy: the negative side. No, that list does not make up *The Bill of Rights*. One might come to that conclusion regarding the way some people act in today's society. That list of attributes makes up the seven deadly sins.

Would these seven items pass through the integrity hub? On which side of the leadership lifeline would those attributes land? When a person reads about this list of seven behaviors, the incorrect story is that they came from the *Bible*. The *Bible* validates them, but nowhere are they recorded in a list like this, and nowhere in the *Bible* are they expressly referred to as the seven deadly sins. Pope Gregory I compiled this list around the year 600 AD.

Gregory also compiled a list of the seven virtues: faith, hope, charity, justice, prudence, temperance, and fortitude, contrasting the seven sins. Do you know who else created a contrasting list of virtues and non-virtues? Buddha, through the four noble truths, and Lao Tzu, through the yin, yang principle. A yin and yang exist for everything.

If the concepts of "good" or "right" didn't exist, then we would not know what constitutes "bad" or "wrong." If I asked you which side faith, hope, charity, justice, prudence, temperance, and fortitude exist, the answer is easy—the positive side.

When we apply things to the leadership lifeline, we can quickly identify when certain things fall on the positive or negative sides. On which side do responsibility and discipline fall? On which side do blame and neglect fall? We quickly knew the answers to those two questions.

On which side does risk fall? Risk can fall on both sides depending on how you view risk. We see this in Aristotle's list of extreme virtues when he addresses greed. The minute you are born, risk exists. Driving to work is risky. Asking someone out on a date is risky. You could get turned down. Going into business is risky.

Want to know how risky life is? You're not going to get out alive. Leadership is not about risk, yet "risk leadership" is one of hundreds of misguided leadership labels. Take an action; there is a risk. Do not take action; there is a risk. Life is one big risk.

How about guilt? On which side of the Leadership Lifeline would you place guilt? Is guilt a negative thing because it implies wrongdoing? Sure it is. It is built into our biology. It is one of nature's ways of telling us we have done wrong. We *feel guilty*.

In the movie *You've Got Mail,* we see a perfect example of the guilt nature embedded in our genes. Joe Fox, played by Tom Hanks, has the ability to zing people when he is provoked, meaning he can belittle them and make them feel inadequate or inferior. Kathleen Kelly, played by Meg Ryan, says she is jealous because she isn't good at acting in this manner. Joe Fox tells her that those zingers are due to some of his worst traits: arrogance, spite, and condescension. Then he warns her. When you act this way, be prepared; remorse will inevitably follow.

Remorse is a form of guilt, an emotion supplied by nature. This built-in mechanism of guilt can prevent us from continuing to act in ways unbecoming a leader. Therefore, we can deduce that guilt is a positive thing. That is, until we see someone use guilt to influence others to do something they did not want to do, guilt becomes a negative thing.

You influenced someone to jump off a fifty-foot cliff, not for money, but because you told them if they didn't, they weren't a real man like the others who have done it. You have guilted someone into doing something. Now, where would you place guilt on the Leadership Lifeline? It exists on both sides.

How about shame? Where would you place that on the Leadership Lifeline? Again, nature provides us with some guidance. We *feel shame* for a reason. That reason is that we know we have done something unleaderly. In this case, shame falls on the positive side. That emotion exists for a reason. We can also shame someone else into doing things. Then, it falls on the negative side. It can fall on both sides of the leadership lifeline.

When testing against the BASIC Leadership platform, we will encounter concepts like risk, guilt, and shame that seem to elude us. But when we look more closely at them, we discover that "the application of each" determines whether they represent the negative or positive side.

Brené Brown, the author of *Daring Greatly* (2012) and *dare to lead* (2018), goes deep into the concept of shame.

> *When perfectionism is driving us, shame is riding*
> *shotgun and fear is that annoying back seat driver.*
> ~Brené Brown

Brené combines perfection, shame, and fear all in one quote. When a person attempts to achieve perfection, what is that a form of? Very good. You're catching on. Trying to achieve perfection is a form of escalation.

In Brown's quote, the attribute of fear falls on the negative side, as does shame. We fear being unable to achieve perfection, when perfection is impossible. It's a set-up, a guarantee to lose that battle. It's self-inflicted by a mindset learned through societal propaganda.

Nothing is perfect, and no one should try to be. When we lose at our attempt for perfection, shame can be, and usually is the result. It's self-inflicted. However, rather than seeking perfection, we can progress toward the best possible version of ourselves. Doing so requires acting in leadership.

> *Practice does not makes perfect. Practice make permanent.* ~Proverb, Unknown

When we act in leadership, shame dissipates. It diminishes in several ways. First, we stop doing things we might be ashamed of, like lying, stealing, and making bad health and financial decisions. Second, by not letting what others might say or think about us impact us.

Others do not have the ability to shame us. We give them the ability and power when we allow what they say to impact how we feel and then act on those feelings.

> *Sticks and stones may break my bones, but words can never hurt me.*

This phrase appears in multiple articles in the 1800s. One such source is *Reasons for adopting the rational system of medicine*, by F. R. Horner, M.D., published in the Northern Times (Liverpool, Lancashire, England), on Thursday, July 23rd, 1857. The exact wording is, "Sticks and stones (says the schoolboy's rhyme) may break men's bones, but bad names will not hurt me."

More than those who hate you, more than
all your enemies, an undisciplined mind does
greater harm. ~Buddha, The Dhammapada[1]

We cannot control what others say and do, but we get to control how we react to what other say and do. Here is a current day quote of the sticks and stones analogy.

You cannot control what happens to you, but you can
control your attitude toward what happens to you.
~Brian Tracy

Once we gain some insight, our perception can quickly change. We have control over more than we think we do, especially where our beliefs are concerned. Remember, nature induced us with the emotion of shame, not so we could be shamed, but so we become aware when we do not act in leadership. Buddha was very specific about both aspects of shame.

Those who are ashamed of deeds they
should not be ashamed of, and not ashamed
of deeds they should be ashamed of, follow
false doctrines on the downward course.
    ~Buddha, The Dhammapada[2]

For some reason, we have been brainwashed to think that living simply, within our means, humbly, and not in pursuit of fame, recognition, and material things that we cling to as a representation of ourselves should be shameful.

We associate our worth with material things and status in a society. Have you ever reached a certain level of status and then lost it? Did you feel shame? I have. Why?

At the age of fifty, I lost everything, at least materially, filed for bankruptcy, and had my home foreclosed. I wanted to hide from everyone. Notice that I said I lost everything and then added "at least materially." You see, it was escalation, pride, recognition, and material possessions, sometimes driven by envy of what others had. I associated myself with what I owned and my position or status in society. That is not what or who we are.

I felt shame over losing a house, why? I was still me. I still had value as a person. That did not change. No one can take that away. If I had remained in a state of shame and depression and lost all hope, then you would not be reading this book right now.

All of that was self-inflicted. Like millions of others, I was living a life of escalation. I thought I needed those things, when I did not. I associated who I was with what I had. Then, when I lost it, shame and guilt resulted, when neither should have existed.

The fact is, I no longer go there in the first place because I now understand I have complete control over it, and it takes consistent practice to avoid it. This is a never-ending progression toward a worthy ideal.

I no longer care about material things. Please do not mistake that personal philosophy to mean that I will not add value to society or have a job, a place to live, a car, or other material things.

I don't care what others think of the car I drive. I do not care about fashion trends and being relevant in terms of some marketing propaganda that tells me who I should be, what I should do, wear, eat, or where to live. My brother Jim and I have a saying now, "It's just stuff."

If I lost it all again, I would not let shame and guilt set in. It's just stuff. It's too bad someone didn't instill this philosophy in us at a much younger age. Certainly not our parents. I'll spare you that life story. Terrible parenting, but certainly not what others around the globe have experienced and are still experiencing today. Human trafficking, modern-day slavery, war-torn countries, famine, to name a few. What a world we would have if more people acted in leadership.

Our world has worked this way for a very long time, and some warned us. Taoism, Buddhism, Greek Philosophy, and the *Bible*, all give us the same insights. Thousands of miles apart, with different cultures and languages,, yet they all arrived at the same place philosophically. Can they all be wrong?

Starting in the mid-1800s, into the mid-1900s, leadership became heavily associated with the top positions in hierarchies. A revival in the 1980s and 1990s tried to bring acting in leadership to the forefront.

It ended up being labeled as personal development. What a disservice to the concept of acting in leadership in its true essence.

How did the character of Joe Fox in the movie *You've Got Mail* conclude that he acted wrongly? Nature built these safety mechanisms into us, both physically through the chemicals our bodies release and emotionally through our brains.

He acted, and then he gained insight into the impact those specific actions had on him and others. He had a habit of acting in a particular manner, which progressed over time.

He didn't pop out of the womb acting like that. It was a progression that developed and became a habit. New insight changed his mindset and beliefs. He then began working on progressing in a different direction—a progression on the positive side of the leadership lifeline.

In his first encounters with Kathleen Kelly, he was arrogant, spiteful, and condescending. Later, when he meets her face to face again, she "zings" him, attacking his character and acting in a condescending manner herself. He sits quietly and patiently, not responding to her insults. He politely excuses himself and leaves without returning any zingers.

This interaction was a collaboration between the two of them and nature, which installed the "guilt" program into our human systems. The Kathleen Kelly character now experienced guilt and remorse for her actions. The roles reversed.

The revised actions of Joe Fox have begun a progression of existing on the positive side of the leadership lifeline. The progression of acting in leadership cannot take place without passing through the integrity hub and landing on the positive side of the leadership lifeline. Because leadership became heavily associated with the top position in hierarchies, we began to treat the symptoms of not acting in leadership, rather than the root causes. Joe Fox began treating the root cause of his guilt.

Now he must consistently act in such a manner that acting in leadership becomes a habit.

CHAPTER TWENTY-SIX

Our Subconscious and Our Habits

The Subconscious Mind

It's odd that today, we have scientific proof related to our habits and our subconscious mind, and it all mirrors the same things the early philosophers enlightened us about regarding both concepts. Yet, it is relatively unknown even within the mass populations of well-developed first-world countries.

Dr. Bruce Lipton spent 30 years working on the subject of Beliefs. From 1987 to 1992, Lipton conducted studies about Beliefs at both Penn State and Stanford University Medical Center. In 2005, he published his book *The Biology of Belief: Unleashing the Power of Consciousness, Matter & Miracles.*

Incredible advancements in technologies regarding how physics works within our bodies and our minds helped Lipton tie together the physical connection and mental connection to address how our beliefs form and how our beliefs impact our behaviors.

I love the example Lipton provides to illustrate how our subconscious mind works. What we are taught and the behaviors we learn are loaded into our subconscious mind. Think of our mind as the operating system of a computer. It's loaded onto the hard drive, then it operates in the background unnoticed. As I'm typing this sentence, my brain is running multiple operations in the background and doing so on autopilot.

Our brains operate like computers. Programs are running in the background on the hard drive of our minds. For instance, auto spell check is running on my laptop computer as I write this book—cool. I like that one. It's not perfect, but it's helpful. Wait, there's a virus operating in the background stealing all my personal stuff? Let's get rid of that one. We can alter the programs on our computers—add some, remove some. We can do that with our subconscious minds.

Let's say you were taught as a child to make sure the cap is put back on a tube of toothpaste. This is a trivial thing. Yet, when we find that someone else left that cap laying there next to the sink with toothpaste dribbling out onto the counter, for some of us, it pushes an emotional button. Why?

As Lipton puts it, "You've just experienced the simple stimulus-response of a behavior program stored in the subconscious mind." A subconscious reaction to a trivial thing. To a *trivial thing?* Yes.

Not only is what we learn in the early stages of our lives significant, but all of that stored data is being used by some autopilot system deep in our brains to do the exact things we want to avoid.

Aristotle, the student of Plato and Socrates, is attributed to the saying, "Give me a child until he is seven and I will show you the man." Aristotle understood this philosophy approximately 2,350 years before Lipton's research. It's incredible just how accurate Aristotle was without using all the scientific instruments that exist today.

Lipton's early work set the stage for providing evidence that this statement is correct. Lipton based his work on what we know today as EEG, which stands for electroencephalogram. The electroencephalogram is a recording of the electrical activity of the brain. The recorded waveforms reflect the cortical electrical activity. Science shows we have four levels of consciousness. Here is how they break down.

- ✓ Delta: Unconscious mind. Age 0 to 2
- ✓ Theta: Imagination state. Ages 3 to 6
- ✓ Alpha: Calm, conscious mind. Ages 7 to 12
- ✓ Beta: Active conscious mind. Age 13 and up

Science has proven that the first two layers, the unconscious mind, and the imagination state, create the basis for our initial habits, which happens in the first seven years. Can you hear the theme music from the Twilight Zone TV series playing in the background?

The subconscious mind processes information at 40 million bits per second, and our conscious mind processes information at 40 bits per second. This means that our subconscious mind operates in the background, controlling between 95% and 99% of our daily actions, and doing this "on autopilot."

It easily overrides our conscious mind, and we are not even aware that it is happening. Our subconscious mind is always in the past or the future and rarely "in the now." We try to predict and establish happiness based on our past experiences, of which we retain tiny bits and pieces, and on a future, we try to envision based on nothing more than what we hope will happen or not happen.

Habits

The Story of Philosophy: The Lives and Opinions of the World's Greatest Philosophers, written by Will Durant, and published in 1991, contains the following sentence.

> *We are what we repeatedly do. Excellence, then, is not an act but a habit.*[1]

You've seen this quote attributed to Aristotle. In Nicomachean Ethics, ii, 4, Aristotle says, "These virtues are formed in man by his doing the actions." Durant takes the more extensive compilation of what Aristotle says and rephrases it in a way that allows us to understand that deeper context. Again, we see that

Aristotle and others understood the concept of habits and how they are formed.

In the Dhammapada, Buddha enlightened us about good and bad habits.

If you do what is evil, do not repeat it or take
pleasure in making it a habit. An evil habit will cause
nothing but suffering. If you do what is good,
keep repeating it and take pleasure in making it a
habit. A good habit will cause nothing but joy.
~Buddha, *The Dhammapada*[2]

In the *Tao Te Ching*, Lao Tzu tells us how non-righteous repeated practices and habits are formed. He called them rituals.

When righteousness is lost there are rituals.
Rituals are the end of fidelity and honesty,
and the beginning of confusion.
~Lao Tzu, Tao Te Ching[3]

In 2012, Charles Duhigg released his book *The Power of Habit*. The book's premise is, "Why we do what we do in life and business." Duhigg's work compiles years of study on the formation of habits. Duhigg helps us dive into what he refers to as our "keystone habits."

Three things define how our habits form and how we can change them.

- Cue
- Routine
- Reward

We only have to see a cookie jar on the counter; that's the cue. Our reward is the yummy taste we experience when we eat it. You want one now, don't you?

Simply reading about a cookie jar triggers a cue. That cue and reward become routine. You have now learned about how habits can be formed, and you also know that this cue, routine, and reward sequence operates in the background in our subconscious mind.

I know that's just one book. What the heck does that guy know, right? In 2018, James Clear published *Atomic Habits: Tiny Changes, Remarkable Results.* Want to take a stab at Clear's findings? It's the same premise using four simple and similar components to habit formation.

- Que
- Craving
- Response
- Reward

James Clear quotes the *Tao Te Ching* in his book. At the time I wrote this chapter, *Atomic Habits* had sold over 15 million copies, and *The Power of Habit* had sold over 10 million copies. The number of books sold illustrates the human desire to learn about why we do what we do. Combine that with Dr. Bruce Lipton's works regarding our subconscious mind, and we have our answer. We arrive at the summation of Aristotle's understanding of habits as stated by Will Durant.

We are what we repeatedly do. Excellence, then, is not an act but a habit. ~Will Durant

Charles Duhigg and James Clear also provide part of the remedy for the root causes of our behaviors, which drive us to not act in leadership.

Excellence is not about making radical changes but about accruing small improvements over time. ~James Clear

The early philosophers also gave us this same advice about small improvements over time. They enlightened us on the concept of a lifelong progression toward a worthy ideal. We think what Duhigg and Clear tell us is some new radical insight. It is not. Here are two examples: one from the *Tao* and one from the *Bible*.

The most difficult in the world
Must be easy in the beginning.
The biggest in the world
Is smallest in the beginning.
So, the sage never strives for greatness,
And can therefore accomplish greatness.
    ~Lao Tzu, *Tao Te Ching*[4]

Do not be deceived: God cannot be mocked. A man reaps what he sows. Whoever sows to please their flesh, from the flesh will reap destruction; whoever sows to please the Spirit, from the Spirit will reap eternal life. Let us not become weary in doing good, for at the proper time we will reap a harvest if we do not give up. ~Galatians 6:7-9 (NIV)[5]

If you were to read the *Bible* passage in Galatians from the Apostle Paul, one of the Disciples of Jesus, would you understand how it instructs us on how habits are formed and the end result of those actions?

Input = output. Do not become weary of small daily habits, for they will eventually yield a great harvest.

Through the *Tao Te Ching*, Lao Tzu tells us how small daily habits create our lives in the long term. Little, seemingly insignificant things done daily lead to big things. What we must understand is that this works in both directions, both positive and negative. We're learning to address the root causes, not treat the symptoms.

Humans possess something no other animal does: the ability to reason and to control our environment, at least to some degree. We get to choose. What are you choosing? What do you believe about any of this? Those beliefs will drive your actions, and those actions will be a progression toward something either positive or negative. In either case, you are forming habits, and only through habits associated with acting in leadership will you arrive at excellence.

Are you beginning to believe that acting in leadership in its true essence is tied to the second definition of leadership under the BASIC Leadership blueprint and has nothing to do with a position in any hierarchy, doing business, acquiring followers, influencing others, or most of the other 800+ misguided leadership labels being presented today?

CHAPTER TWENTY-SEVEN

Backward In Time

So much of what the early philosophers understood around the 5th century B.C. has been quoted in different variations for hundreds of years. Let's work our way backward in time and look at some examples. The first two quotes address being grateful and having gratitude.

Be thankful for what you have; you'll end up having more. If you concentrate on what you have, you will never ever have enough. ~Oprah Winfrey

Life is sweeter when you have an attitude of gratitude. ~Dolly Parton

The following two quotes address how, as individuals, it is us who must change, not the circumstances or others.

I always get to where I'm going by walking away from where I've been. ~A.A. Milne, Winnie the Pooh

If you change the way you look at things, the things you look at change. ~Wayne Dyer

We see a quote by Wayne Dyer, a popular self-help author and motivational speaker who teaches the same principles as an iconic cartoon character. We also see how Dolly Parton, a famous singer, and Oprah Winfrey, a famous talk show host, both practice gratitude.

I could provide hundreds of more recent quotes from people of all ethnicities and genders from the most recent two decades. Those quotes address gratitude, greed, peace of mind, integrity, and a multitude of philosophical ideals.

Moving back a bit in time, during the 1980s, a revival seemed to begin, quickly growing and exploding in the 1990s with authors and speakers such as Zig Ziglar, Brian Tracy, Suze Orman, Tony Robbins, Wayne Dyer, Susan Powter, Larry Winget, John Maxwell, Stephen Covey, Martha Beck, and Jim Rohn. This era was, and still is, labeled personal development or self-growth. Businesses clamored to get these gurus to speak at their organizations and conferences. Most of what these gurus offer mirrors the teachings of Lao Tzu, Buddha, Greek philosophers, and Jesus.

So many people are continuing to join in on this movement that I can't keep track and no longer recognize all the names. It's a multi-billion dollar industry. This proves the immense desire for what the early philosophers taught thousands of years ago.

Just before the late 19th-century explosion of personal development, we had Napoleon Hill, Dale

Carnegie, James Allen, Louise Hay, Maya Angelou, Viktor Frankl, Bob Proctor, and Earl Nightingale. Do you recognize any of those names?

> *Whatever we plant in our subconscious mind and nourish with repetition and emotion will one day become a reality.* ~Earl Nightingale

> *I do not fix problems. I fix my thinking. Then, problems fix themselves.* ~Louise Hay

> *If you don't like something, change it. If you can't change it, change your attitude.* ~Maya Angelou

Eleanor Roosevelt was the longest-serving first lady of the United States from 1933 to 1945, during her husband, President Franklin D. Roosevelt's four terms in office. The two-term limit for presidents was not yet in place; it began in 1947. Eleanor is often quoted for her philosophical wisdom.

> *You can often change your circumstances by changing your attitude.* ~Eleanor Roosevelt

Prior to the early to mid-1900s group, we had the late 1800s to early 1900s New Thought Movement. William Walker Atkinson, Prentice Mulford, Bruce MacLelland, Wallace D. Wattles, and James Allen, who wrote *As A Man Thinketh*, published in 1901, are included in that group. Those names will not likely ring a bell to most people, even those of my generation. I was born in 1961.

In December 1901, William Atkinson became the editor of *New Thought* magazine, a very popular publication. The New Thought Movement wasn't about new ideas. It was about our thoughts, the law of attraction, and success or failure based on what we believe.

> *A man is literally what he thinks, his character being the complete sum of all his thoughts.* ~James Allen

> "Fear is the parent of *worry, hate, jealousy, malice, anger, discontent, failure* – and all the rest. The man who rids himself of fear will find that the rest of the brood have disappeared. *The only way to be free is to get rid of fear.* Tear it out by the roots." ~William Walker Atkinson

How to act in leadership is all over the place, spanning time and cultures. No matter the timeline, age, race, ethnicity, or gender, we gravitate toward those who show us how to act in leadership.

A parable, *The Tale of the Two Wolves*, helps us understand the power of our beliefs. Whatever we input is what we output.

> *One evening, an elderly Cherokee mentor told his grandson about a battle that goes on inside people. He said, "There is a battle going on inside of me. It is a terrible fight between two wolves. One wolf is evil. He is made up of anger, envy, sorrow, regret, greed, arrogance, self-pity, guilt, resentment, inferiority, lies, false pride, superiority, and ego."*

> *He continued, "The other is good – he is joy, peace, love, hope, serenity, humility, kindness, benevolence, empathy, generosity, truth, compassion, and faith.*

The same fight is going on inside you and inside every other person, too." The grandson thought about it for a minute and then asked his grandfather, "Which wolf will win?" The elder, wise grandfather replied, "The one that you feed."

The story of the two wolves is a popular legend of unknown origin. It is sometimes attributed to the Lenape or Cherokee people, indigenous to the US. It probably dates from the 1700s or 1800s, but no one truly knows.

There were women philosophers such as Hypatia who lived in Egypt around 400 AD. Despite what some believe, women played key roles in history when it comes to acting in leadership. We saw earlier examples with Suze Orman, Susan Powter, and Eleanor Roosevelt.

Moving back 400 years before Hypatia, we arrive at the teachings of Jesus, recorded by his disciples and others as part of the *Bible.*

Aesop's Fables, or the Aesopica, is a collection of fables credited to Aesop, a slave and storyteller who lived in ancient Greece between 620 and 564 B.C. *One of Aesop's fables, The Boy Who Cried Wolf,* teaches us what can happen when we repeatedly lie.

What I love about the written version of many of Aesop's fables is that the person who does not act in leadership is an ass (a donkey).

When philosophers such as Plato and Aristotle wanted to take a jab at those who ruled in high places, they would use these fables to make their point. Because they told a parable, a story using animal characters to make their point, the person telling the story was not punished as if they actually told a person of power that they were acting like an ass.

When I grew up, there were only three TV channels. Aesop and Son was a series of shorts that appeared on The Rocky and Bullwinkle Show from 1959 to 1962 and then in syndication for a period of time thereafter. A total of thirty-nine five-minute episodes were produced. Each episode taught a lesson. I wonder how many of the newer generations know of Aesop. Albert Einstein understood and had a solid opinion on children's parables that teach lessons in leadership.

If you want your children to be intelligent, read them fairy tales. If you want them to be more intelligent, read them more fairy tales. ~ Albert Einstein

Ahhh, a trip down memory lane. Aesop's fables reminded me of the Rocky and Bullwinkle show. I distinctly remember an episode where the villain Natasha says to Boris, "That is great plan Boris, but it still does not solve problem of Moose and Squirrel." You can use this line when someone at work offers a solution that does not solve the actual problem and addresses the symptoms, not the root cause. The key is to say it using a villainous Russian accent.

History is rich and deep with leadership lessons. That brings us back to where we started: Taoism, Buddhism, Greek Philosophy, and the teachings of the *Bible*.

Our beliefs lead the way, followed by acting in accordance with those beliefs. Progressing toward acting in leadership is a lifelong pursuit, a worthy ideal. All the while, we gain insight into how to continue that progression. And it will take all of us together to accomplish it. Not perfection, not paradise, but continued betterment, one person at a time. And it starts with you, not with someone else.

During the 2023 Global Leadership Summit, GLS, Dick DeVoss, a former CEO of Amway, interviewed Condoleezza Rice, the 66th Secretary of State. What does Rice have to say? A lot. Here is one of her many quotes and philosophies.

> *There are no victims. When you consider yourself a victim, you have given control of your life to somebody else. And you may not be able to control your circumstances, but you can control your response to your circumstances.* ~Condoleezza Rice

Does that quote look familiar? It resembles a quote by Brian Tracy from an earlier chapter.

> *You cannot control what happens to you, but you can control your attitude toward what happens to you.* ~Brian Tracy

I will revise Tracy's quote to the following.

> *You cannot control what happens, but you can control your attitude toward what happens.* ~Scott M. Carter

Things do not happen *to us*. Most of life just happens. How often have you said or heard someone say, "Why does this always keep happening to me," Or some variation of this statement? When we raise our awareness and gain insight, we can begin our progression of acting in leadership.

The teachings of Taoism tell us that things do not happen to us. We must go with the flow and let go of that mindset. Only then can we be in harmony. Life will happen, not to us, but with us.

Good and bad exist for all of us. That's how the world works. The four noble truths of Buddhism tell us the same thing. Most of our suffering is self-inflicted. Those things do not happen *to us*.

> *By oneself is evil done; by oneself one is injured. Do not do evil, and suffering will not come. Everyone has the choice to be pure or impure. No one can purify another.*
> ~Buddha, The Dhammapada[1]

Greek philosophers enlightened us on how the world works. The world does not make things personal. We imagine that when something happens to us, the world is somehow against us. As if nature and the universe do it intentionally to us. We have that viewpoint when it's about us. However, we view it differently when it impacts someone else, not us.

> *It is absurd to make external circumstances responsible and not oneself, and to make oneself responsible for noble acts and pleasant objects responsible for base ones.*
> ~Aristotle, *Nicomachean Ethics*[2]

All of this is easy when we have the context to accompany the quotes. This whole time, we've been gaining insight and raising our awareness.

CHAPTER TWENTY-EIGHT

Awareness

Somewhere, a village is missing their idiot.

In our twenties, when one of our friends did something we considered *not so bright*, we'd look at them and utter those words. "Somewhere, a village is missing their idiot." Most people think this refers to IQ, a person's measure of intelligence. That is partly true.

Usually, when it was said about me, it was about awareness. I have no idea what my IQ is because I've never taken a test. I can tell you that I took a series of six calculus math classes in college—yes, six levels of calculus mathematics, then onto mathematics theory.

On test days, I was known as "that guy." After 20 minutes, I'd meander to the front of the room, hand my completed exam to the professor, stroll out the door, and get 100 out of 100 as a grade. Yep, I was that guy. By the way, all that means is that I was good at memorizing stuff and effectively regurgitating information without letting stress and anxiety block my ability to do so. That's college in a nutshell.

I could do that really well, but boy-oh-boy, I could be an absolute idiot when it came to awareness. I use the wording "could be" because a person can increase their awareness. It's like any other skill set, such as input, output, and our habits. Once a person is aware of awareness, they can work on it.

Awareness

Knowledge is one thing; awareness is something totally different. Awareness is the state of being conscious or mindful of something, while knowledge is the information one possesses.

> *Those who understand others are clever,*
> *Those who understand themselves are wise.*
> *Those who defeat others are strong,*
> *Those who defeat themselves are mighty.*
> ~Lao Tzu, *Tao Te Ching*[1]

Being aware of one's own shortcomings makes a person wise. Changing one's trajectory to acting in leadership defeats the non-acting in leadership side of oneself, which makes one mighty.

> *Learn what is right; then teach others, as*
> *The wise do. Before trying to guide others, be your*
> *Own guide first. It is hard to learn to guide oneself.*
> ~Buddha, *The Dhammapada*[2]

Yes, the lessons include teaching others, but only once we have mastered the lessons ourselves. Misguidedly, holding others accountable to goals set in the process of doing business led us to believe that leadership is about holding others accountable. When everyone holds themselves accountable, then the need to hold others accountable dissipates.

Remember, "Know Thyself" was one of the maxims on the entry to the temple of Apollo.

> *Do not judge, or you too will be judged. For in the same way you judge others, you will be judged, and with the measure you use, it will be measured to you.*
>
> *Why do you look at the speck of sawdust in your brother's eye and pay no attention to the plank in your own eye? How can you say to your brother, 'Let me take the speck out of your eye,' when all the time there is a plank in your own eye? You hypocrite, first take the plank out of your own eye, and then you will see clearly to remove the speck from your brother's eye.*
> ~Matthew 7:1-5 (NIV)[3]

Matthew 7:1-5 is part of the sermon on the mount by Jesus. That sermon contains many lessons for acting in leadership, including judging yourself first and foremost.

When we become aware, which is done by gaining insight through actions, all aspects of how one acts in leadership become very clear.

In 2009, Jean Greaves and Travis Bradberry published their book *Emotional Intelligence 2.0*. What is this book about? Our awareness. Greaves and Bradberry provide insight into an awareness quotient, referred to as EQ, rather than an IQ number. They help us understand the difference between knowledge and awareness.

Greaves and Bradberry were not the first to discover this concept, but they were the first to put it in such simple terms that even I could understand it and act on it.

Daniel Goleman's book *Emotional Intelligence: Why it can matter more than IQ* was published in 1995. Dr. Eliot wasn't the only one to warn us about stress-related heart disease.

Gathering scientific data from 101 studies, Goleman tells us that people who have chronic anxiety, anger, stress, cynicism (distrust in people's motives), and pessimism (negative thoughts) were found to have double the risk of disease. Those ailments include, but are not limited to, asthma, arthritis, headaches, peptic ulcers, and heart disease.

Goleman says distressing emotions are as toxic for heart disease as smoking or high cholesterol, and that list of things is a significant threat to our health. That's knowledge or information. Your EQ, Emotional Quotient, is about your awareness of the level of anxiety, stress, anger, pessimism, cynicism, and other similar things that you exhibit so you can do something about it.

EQ is the modern term encompassing all that the early philosophers told us about awareness and our emotions. Goleman provides methods for addressing the root causes of stress, anxiety, and many of the other negative aspects of the Leadership Lifeline.

Just because a person has a high IQ doesn't mean they also have a high level of awareness. A person with a high IQ can also have a high level of emotional intelligence, but the two do not automatically go hand in hand.

Awareness... one mouth, two eyes, and two ears. Nature told us that we should look and listen twice as much as we speak and only speak when what we say is worth saying. Let's face it: some things are better left unsaid. But, if you're like me, I generally realize this after I have already said them. Then, I spend the next five minutes trying to remove my foot from my mouth.

All men are capable of self-knowledge and moderation. ~Heraclitus

Heraclitus lived before Socrates, just as the seven sages attributed to the Greek Delphi maxims. Many quotes that address self-awareness use the wording self-knowledge to address understanding one's self.

In one of Greaves and Bradberry's studies, the people in business with the lowest EQ levels were CEOs, followed by top executives. That begs us to ask the question of whether we are missing a very important component that should be taught in business schools.

EQ Is Simple

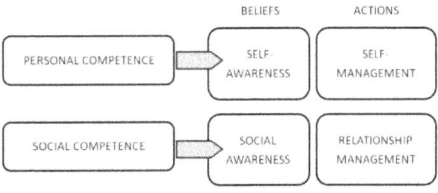

We begin with personal competence. You might be competent at your job or with your knowledge of a particular subject, but how competent are you regarding your awareness of your beliefs and actions and how those actions determine the trajectory of your life and the impact you have on those around you?

In college, I was competent in calculus math but not so much in my awareness of acting in leadership. I have worked diligently to change that – First, to conquer myself.

> *Victory over oneself is of all victories the first and finest.* ~Plato, *Laws, Book 1, 626e*

We put self-awareness under the label of personal development, and somehow, that translated into some form of selfishness because it was, first and foremost, about ourselves. Nothing could be farther from that misguided mindset.

Maslow's Hierarchy of Needs shows us that the highest level is self-awareness. Abraham Maslow first wrote *Eupsychian Management: A Journal,* published in 1965. Most people know it under a revised name, *Maslow on Management*, republished in 1998. Maslow takes the same philosophies we've been talking about in relation to leadership and lays out the process for implementing them into business.

The entire pyramid he presents is about understanding the progression of developing ourselves, meeting our basic needs, and progressing toward enlightenment. Enlightenment? Yes, it's simply about reaching a higher level of self-awareness.

When we travel by airplane, what do they instruct us to do in the event of an emergency? They tell us to put on our own oxygen masks first. Why? What's the purpose of that "take care of yourself first" approach?

The answer is: You are of little use to others if you run out of oxygen yourself. It is a metaphor. The real lesson is that we should not wait for an emergency to begin putting on our own oxygen masks, metaphorically speaking.

You cannot tell others they should be more aware, to be more mindful, and not practice it yourself. It's like a fat doctor who smokes while gulping down pastries and then giving advice on how to live a healthy life.

Be the change you want to see in the world. ~Mahatma Gandi

If you want to help others, act in leadership first. Be the example. We run around judging others, criticizing others, and at the same time, we are what we have been criticizing. How silly.

In chapter twenty-one, *Divergent & Manusmriti*, we learned a bit about personality profiles. The Myers–Briggs Personality test separates us into sixteen categories. The Myers-Briggs platform sprang from the works of Carl G. Jung in the 1920s. Jung developed the four personality types we see in the DiSC personality profile testing, Dominance—Influence—Steadiness--Conscientiousness.

These platforms provide a great way for us to learn why we predominantly act the way we do so we may better interact with others in society. It's about working on our own traits that are not conducive to leadership.

In 2024, we tell people that leadership is about holding others accountable. When we look back at all the lessons provided thousands of years ago, we see that this approach is misguided.

That's why some are attempting to correct this misguided belief in business. In 2000, Tom Coens and Mary Jenkins published their book *Abolishing Performance Appraisals: Why They Backfire and What To Do Instead*. They carried forward their studies from the works of W. Edwards Deming, who published *Out of the Crisis* in 1982. Demings' work gives us fourteen points of management from his decades of studying why the Japanese kicked butt in manufacturing in the last half of the 1900s. They didn't do performance appraisals as we know them today.

Holy blunders, Batman. We got that whole "leadership is about holding others accountable" wrong. That's part of the misunderstood "carrot and stick" method of motivational approaches from the early 1900s. "Stick" refers to punishment as a motivational tool. "Carrot" refers to rewards, monetary incentives, used to motivate people in business. If you wan to learn about the pitfalls and real impact of sticks and carrot motivation, read Daniel Pink's book, *Drive*, Published in 2009

Show us your plan for addressing your shortcomings and self-improvement and how you have achieved that goal of personal perfection, and perhaps we will give you a pass on critiquing and judging others. The irony is that when you act in leadership, not judging others is part of the process. It will be a life-long progression, so we will expect no more judgments or criticisms from you, madam or sir.

Act in leadership by raising your level of awareness. It's time to raise your awareness about the practical application of acting in leadership.

CHAPTER TWENTY-NINE

Practical Application

In the 2002 version of the movie *The Time Machine*, Dr. Alexander Hartdegen invents a machine to travel back in time and change the circumstances surrounding the death of the woman he loves.

Due to the paradox of time travel, every attempt to keep her from dying creates a new way in which she meets her demise. Rather than focus on saving her, he begins seeking a solution to this time travel paradox by heading into the future in search of an answer.

At one point during his journey into the future, Alexander enters a library and has a conversation with a hologram. This holographic person consists of a computer program containing the concise, detailed information about all human knowledge.

Alexander asks the holographic man about time travel. The hologram responds with a sigh, as if he's actually human, and sarcastically offers up the category of science fiction and books such as the H.G. Wells novel *The Time Machine*. Alexander responds by saying, "No, no. Practical application." The library hologram tells him time travel, in terms of practical application, does not exist.

Alexander continues to move forward hundreds of thousands of years, and the two characters meet again. This time, the hologram says he remembers his conversation with Alexander about time travel and its practical application. The hologram, who thought time travel wasn't possible, now realizes it has become a reality. Here are my questions to you, the reader.

Do you think the practical application of acting in leadership can become a reality? Yes, but only if acting in leadership can be defined. Do you believe it can be defined? Do you believe the BASIC Leadership blueprint helps us determine when a person is acting in leadership?

Blue Zones & Practical Application

Most of us desire to live longer. What if I told you that there are five places in the world where people are known to live longer lives than anyplace else. Would you want to go there?

Dan Buettner, an explorer, award-winning journalist, and producer, discovered the five places in the world where people live the longest, healthiest lives. He dubbed these "the Blue Zones." Since his first publication in 2010, he has produced an entire series of books to enlighten you and me on living longer, healthier lives.

You are not alone if you said you'd like to go there. The *New York Times* Magazine and *National Geographic* printed articles about his research. Since the publication of Buettner's research, those two publications have become the most popular and most read. These are the five blue zone regions.

- Loma Linda, California, United States
- Nicoya Peninsula, Costa Rica
- Sardinia, Italy
- Ikaria, Greece
- Okinawa, Japan

If you were asked the root causes of this incredible longevity, could you tell us? The Blue Zone website says this about the research.

> *Dan Buettner and his team dedicated their research to finding what these people had in common. What they found was nothing extreme; simply a balance of good health habits and social engagement. Buettner listed nine factors, including: moderate, regular physical activity, life purpose, stress reduction, moderate calorie intake, a plant-based diet, moderate alcohol intake, especially wine, engagement in spirituality or religion, engagement in family life, and engagement in social life as the lifestyle habits leading to long, healthy lives.*

Do you see anything in that list about magic waters, advanced medical technologies, or medicines? Do you see anything in that list about genetics, ethnicity, or a predisposition to being healthy based on parents or ancestors?

That list consists of basic, common-sense stuff. We always come back to the basics. Basics and common sense. Who would have thunk? Who and what sources could have ever enlightened us on these crazy, what appears to be secret, hidden-away approaches to a longer, healthier life? Taoism, Buddhism, Greek philosophers, and biblical teachings.

> *Health is the best gift, contentment the best wealth,*
> *trust the best kinsman, nirvana the joy.*
> ~Buddha, *The Dhammapada*[1]

Buddha lets us know health is about both the body and mind. We'll get to the mind, the contentment part in upcoming chapters. Lao Tzu tells us the same thing.

> *He who treasures his body as much as the world*
> *Can care for the world.*
> *Those who defeat others are strong,*
> *He who loves his body as much as the world*
> *Can be entrusted with the world.*
> ~Lao Tzu, *Tao Te Ching*[2]

In today's world, as in all history, we're taking advice from people who don't have their ducks in a row. Doctors and nurses who smoke are telling us how to be healthy. People who are deep in debt are giving us financial advice. And worst of all, unethical politicians are making the rules for how others should behave. Lao Tzu warned us about all of this in five simple sentences.

If a person cannot be trusted to care of their own body, which is the only place they have to live, then how in the world can they be trusted with anything else? That's one of the underlying lessons being taught here.

For physical training is of some value, but godliness has value for all things, holding promise for both the present life and the life to come.
  ~1 Timothy 4:8 (NIV)[3]

Throughout the *Bible*, we see lessons for dealing with the physical body and the mind. The body always follows the mind. Beliefs drive actions. This mind-body connection is why Timothy tells us physical training has some value but is not the primary thing. We'll gain more insight into this in chapters thirty-five and thirty-six.

Eating is not enough to keep a man well; he must also take exercise. ~Hippocrates[4]

Prayer indeed is good, but while calling on the gods a man should lend a hand himself. ~Hippocrates[4]

Have you heard of the Hippocratic Oath? It is administered to young physicians upon entering the medical profession. Hippocrates, a physician, lived from 460 BC to 377 BC. His teachings, along with others, helped to form the Hippocratic Oath. I won't write the entire oath, but it begins with this phrase.

By all that I hold highest, I promise my patients competence, integrity, candor, personal commitment to their best interest, compassion, and absolute discretion, and confidentiality within the law.

Hippocrates tells us, first and foremost, we are responsible for taking action to make things happen. Doctors take an oath to act with integrity, but where is your oath to do the same in your life? Why isn't our entire planet one big blue zone? The issue is that most people will not do what those people do, no matter where they live. What the people do and how they live makes those places seem magical.

We should have a societal Hippocratic oath that would look something like this, along with the teachings of what it means to act in leadership. We need to put practical application into action.

By all that I hold highest, I promise to live my life with integrity and a personal commitment to acting in leadership. ~Scott M. Carter, Leadership Oath

On my way to work one morning, I listened to a popular radio DJ share her story of being enlightened about the blue zones. When I heard the words "blue zone," my face lit up. I thought, "Alright, more people are going to hear about how they can live healthier lives." When she finished, I wanted to yank my steering wheel onto the next off-ramp, pull over, and call the station.

In Okinawa, Japan, one of the things they eat is purple sweet potatoes, rich in antioxidants. The morning DJ went on a hunt for this item and found they were difficult to get and very expensive. To her, the purple potatoes were the answer. She needed those to get started. Because of her story she shared on the radio that morning, I wonder how many people now believed they could not do what those in the blue zones do because of access to Okinawan purple potatoes. The purple sweet potatoes aren't the reason that Okinawa, Japan, is a blue zone.

Okinawans act on their beliefs, their mindset, and a healthy life happens in a slow progression that one does not even notice. These six places do not have anything that you and I do not have access to regarding healthier versions of foods, nor do the people have some special abilities, mentally and physically, that you and I do not possess, no matter where we live.

The people in Nicoya Peninsula, Costa Rica, Sardinia, Italy, and Ikaria, Greece do not have Okinawan purple potatoes.

I did not tell that story to pick on this local DJ. So often, we miss the big picture. Those five zones have no magical air, water, or plant life. You do not need to go there or eat what they eat to live like a blue zone person. If you went there, I doubt you'd do what it takes. It's not the place or a specific food; it's the beliefs, acting on those beliefs, gaining insight from those actions, and progressing toward a worthy ideal.

Buettner and his team can tell you the nine non-magical attributes of a longer, healthier life. Likewise, with one hundred percent certainty, I can tell you the seven non-magical components of the blueprint for acting in leadership.

The hologram in the Time Machine movie realized that a practical application for time travel exists. You're beginning to realize that what Buettner provides and what I provide here are both recipes for *Practical Application.* Let's review the BASIC Leadership blueprint.

- Your beliefs, your mindset, will drive your actions.
- Those actions will create a progression toward a continuous result, good or bad.
- Good or bad depends on whether you act with integrity and on the positive side of the lifeline.
- During that progression, you will gain insight.
- You must use that insight to set your trajectory on the positive side of the leadership lifeline.
- You will collaborate in some form or fashion with nature or others throughout your entire life.
- You will randomly and constantly move from one component to another within the BASIC Leadership outer ring.

Ever heard the phrase, "Art imitates life?" Life also often imitates art.

CHAPTER THIRTY

Art, Life, and Leadership

Someone back in time was doing the things they needed to do to survive. They stopped and mixed in some fun by kicking a ball along the ground. Now we have the game of soccer, European football. It is boring to some and fascinating to others. So many things have been born out of simply having our own personal version of fun.

Roger Penrose, a mathematical physicist with a Ph.D. in algebraic geometry, shared the 2020 Nobel Prize in physics with two others. According to the Nobel Prize website, "Penrose used ingenious mathematical methods to prove that black holes are a direct consequence of Albert Einstein's general theory of relativity."

Einstein himself did not believe that black holes existed. However, January 1965, ten years after

Einstein's death, Penrose proved that black holes could form and described them in detail. I don't know about you, but this guy is way out of my league in mathematics. What do you suppose his idea of fun might be when he is not investigating black holes?

Roger Penrose played around with geometric shapes like the tiles you and I see on the walls and floors in our kitchens and bathrooms. Penrose discovered two shapes that could be used to create an infinite number of patterns without ever repeating the same pattern. For example, you could tile a soccer field without repeating one of the previous patterns.

See what happens when people mix some fun into their lives—we get sports and other fun activities, and we also discover things like the mathematical Penrose Tiling system. But why am I talking about Roger Penrose and infinite tiling patterns in a leadership book? Great question.

It was 1974 when Penrose discovered the tiling system, which would be named after him. Decades after Penrose presented his findings on this infinite pattern tiling system, a Harvard physicist named Peter Lu was visiting Uzbekistan, a country located in central Asia. Yeah, I had never heard of this country before, until I saw them compete in the Olympics. Don't feel bad.

While in Uzbekistan, Lu encountered a 15th-century building elaborately decorated with tiles. In 2007, Lu published a study showing the pattern as Penrose tiling. Five hundred years before it was named after Penrose, societies were already using forms of this tiling pattern. Uzbekistan isn't the only place. Since Lu's paper, patterns in Egypt, Greece, Australia, and Europe, some of dating back much further, have been identified as Penrose tile patterns.

Now, we can answer the question of what the Penrose tiling system has to do with leadership. In chapters eleven through fourteen, we see similarities between the patterns of Taoism, Buddhism, Greek Philosophy, and the *Bible*.

Do you believe all these societies where the Penrose tiling patterns have been identified somehow had a worldwide geometry convention about non-repeating patterns? No more than China, India, and Greece had a global summit on acting in leadership. It was intrinsic, organic, the natural pattern of life.

It is unnecessary to fill this chapter with quotes from Lao Tzu, Buddha, Greek philosophers, and the *Bible* to illustrate my point. Each chapter of this book provides those examples.

The same components, Beliefs, Actions, a Successful positive progression, Insights gained during that progression, and a Collaboration with nature, the world, or others, exist in each of these cultures as the primary tiles of life in a non-repeating pattern. The BASIC™ Leadership blueprint is the operating manual that shows the alignment.

Like the Penrose Tiling system, life is an infinite, non-repeating pattern. Sure, large behavioral patterns such as humans going to war against one another repeat; that's where we get phrases like "history repeats itself."

However, each of those occurrences does not precisely mirror any previous conflict. Each plays out without repeating the same way as any prior conflict. What happens within the BASIC Leadership blueprint mirrors the Penrose tiling system.

BASIC uses five components, and a person lives within those five components in a never-repeating pattern of life. No two lives are ever lived the same.

Beyond the five components that define how life works, acting in leadership requires passing through the integrity filter and landing on the positive side of the leadership lifeline. The five outer ring components of the BASIC Leadership platform are the Penrose tiles of life.

If someone had approached me seven years ago and told me that I would be writing a chapter about leadership using the Penrose tiling system as an analogy, I would have laughed at them, but only after asking, "What the heck is the Penrose tiling system?"

That is how life works; you cannot predict the next pattern or thing in a system that never repeats. Each pattern has its own beauty, and the next pattern cannot exist without the last pattern and the pattern before it. This unpredictable life pattern is the same wisdom that Lao Tzu, Buddha, Greek Philosophers, and the *Bible* all provide.

We seek predictability and certainty, in a world where that cannot exist at a high level. Attempting to predict everything leads to stress, anxiety, and fear. Acting in leadership helps us assist in the direction of our lives, and we can be more prepared for whatever comes our way, but you and I cannot predict the unpredictable next pattern.

CHAPTER THIRTY-ONE

BASIC™ Health - Acting in Leadership

Practical application for time travel—it's not a reality. Acting in leadership regarding your health? Yes, that exists.

Here are some instructions on what actions to take right now to begin acting in leadership in one part of your life: your physical health. Yes, right now, not later or tomorrow. This "take action now" is the practical application part of this book.

Go to your kitchen, open your fridge, and remove all the junk food and unhealthy items. Next, go to your cupboards, pantry, and any other places you store food and remove all the junk food and unhealthy items.

You don't need to be an expert to begin this process. If you are unsure, leave that item. However, there are things you know you should not eat—pastries,, snacks such as chips, and desserts or candy, which should be self-explanatory. Donate what you can and throw away the rest. Stop right now and do that.

Next, replace the unhealthy items with healthier items. You know what "healthier foods" means. You are intelligent, or you wouldn't be reading this book.

Can't afford healthy food? B.S., Bovine Scat. Here's a little secret, *whispering in your ear*, "It's not the expensive little purple sweet potatoes from Japan." All that crap you've been eating costs as much, if not more, than foods that are better for you. In fact, the price you will pay later due to poor health is far greater.

Chicken, fish, fresh vegetables, and fruits. Short list, right? Oh, you're a vegan? My bad. Get some friggin beans and nuts for your protein intake. Problem solved.

Every time you pick up a package of "ready-to-eat, convenient" food, read the label. If it says fat-free and then has any kind of sugar in it, put it back on the shelf. You've been propagandized to live a busy life and then look for "convenience" to theoretically save time.

Over 56 different variations of sugars are added to our foods: corn syrup, fructose, sucrose, and lactose, just to name a few. It's hard to find a product without some form of sugar.

Remember, the food pyramid was not a health solution, but that does not mean part of it doesn't provide some helpful insight. Sugars = bad. Just say no. Every condiment you dump on food is generally loaded with sugar. Find another way to give your food flavor. I just helped you with more items to remove from your fridge and pantry. You're welcome.

Fat does not equal bad. That's a fallacy. They took all the fats out of foods and loaded them with sugar. There is no higher level of stupidity than whoever came up with that idea. You've been propagandized to believe fat-free = healthy. We need fats in our diet. No, not spooning lard into your yapper like it's a tub of ice cream, or deep frying everything in Crisco. Use fish oils, flaxseed oil, anything omega 3-6-9 related, olive oil, avocado oil, and yes, even a small amount of what have been labeled as bad fats. Your body needs some of those.

What's your next excuse? Allergies? How about wheat allergies and celiac disease? First, if you know you have allergies, take them seriously. People die from being exposed to peanuts if they genuinely have extreme nut allergies. With that said, how can so many people suddenly have celiac disease?

Do you know what a placebo is? It's a pill that has no real medical therapeutic effect. It can be a little pill made out of sugar. In their book, *The Healing Brain: Breakthrough discoveries about how the brain keeps us healthy*, Robert Ornstein and David Sobel provide examples of how people given placebos were cured of their ailments. This outcome is known as the placebo effect.

Now, here's my point. If because you think you are getting a medication and it's a sugar pill, your brain tells your body to cure some minor ailment, how do you suppose your brain works when constantly bombarded with information about all the ailments people are thought to have? It's the reverse of healing.

If a drug company is advertising something, it must be because a ton of people have that issue, right? The little insight light bulb suddenly lit up over your head, right?

If pharmaceutical companies truly wanted people to be healthier, they'd own a large chain of health clubs and market those to people as heavily as they market their drugs.

You're tired after a hard day's work and had a piece of wheat bread for lunch; by God, you must have celiac disease. It seems that every time someone sneezes now, they have some major medical condition.

I provided those last five paragraphs to illustrate a point. So many people now struggle at the grocery store because they believe they can't eat so many things. The reality is that most people who think they have all these little allergies probably don't. It's just like all the other ailments you didn't know you had until you saw the commercial for the pill that can cure what you don't have. You don't exercise, eat like crap, then blame someone or something else.

If you take the pill that addresses the symptoms, you can have diarrhea, vomiting, and blurred vision, but your restless leg syndrome will be cured. Yes, you have restless leg syndrome. It happens in your sleep; you just don't know it. A commercial will soon tell you so. Here's a pill; it's called propagandamycin.

How about some basic food knowledge? A whole grain is exactly what it sounds like: whole. Whole grains have not been broken into the individual components that make up the grain.

For example, wheat, rice, oats, barley, corn, and quinoa have three components.

1) The bran. The thin, fibrous outer layer.
2) The endosperm. The starchy middle layer.
3) The Germ. The core of the grain that germinates when it is planted.

Eat whole-grain rice, typically brown rice and oats, instead of wheat bread of any kind. Enriched grains are refined. Many, if not most, of the natural vitamins are lost, and then they are fortified with additional nutrients. Words like "fortified" and "enriched" make us think it's a healthy option—like we can take things out of nature and effectively put them back.

Buy foods like whole-grain rice instead. Yes, it will take 20 minutes to cook. If that's a hassle for you, then it's a good thing you weren't born before quick food was an option; otherwise, you'd already be dead. Perhaps your life is too busy? Go back and read the progression versus escalation chapter. You've escalated too many things in your life.

What do you think the people in the blue zones believe and act upon regarding food? Do you think they are all running around telling each other they have all these health issues? In Sardinia, eating whole-grain breads is recommended.

Next, get off your butt and move a little. In the blue zones, they refer to it as moderate, regular physical activity. How much moderate physical activity do you have in your life? You eat like crap, don't get much exercise, then when you get home from work, you have no energy, so you plop down on the couch and pick up the remote. I've been there. I still do it from time to time. It takes effort to undo those habits. That's why it's called a progressive realization of a worthy ideal. Getting healthier is a worthy ideal.

You're still waiting for that secret formula, aren't you? The 3 things you need to know to _____ (fill in the blank). The 5 foods that will make you instantly healthy. The workout program where you don't actually have to work out. The newly discovered nutrient you can eat and look like a fitness model in just three weeks, but first, you need to cure your restless leg syndrome.

It's all over the place—TV, radio, pop-up ads, banner ads, text solicitations on our phones, propaganda galore. I'll eat like crap now, not exercise, and take a pill later. That long list of side effects is for other people, not you. Don't worry, you're special (eye roll), or your genetics are the problem, so doing all this won't help (another eye roll). Before starting the next chapter, clean your fridge and cupboards, then head to the store for some healthy options. Park a bit farther away from the door to the store and walk instead of circling the lot, looking for the closest spot. That is acting in leadership.

CHAPTER THIRTY-TWO

Goal Setting For Life

Are you still reading? Or did you take the actions we discussed in the last chapter? Congratulations if you did. I'm betting you didn't because the statistics are accurate. Three out of one hundred people will act on it. You get a pass if you read in bed before going to sleep, so set a goal to do both steps tomorrow.

Here's what I can tell you for sure. If you do not have a legitimate reason for not acting immediately, if you said, "I'll start tomorrow," or some other random day, you won't do anything. It might as well be a New Year's Resolution. Those are a waste of time; they rarely work. Why do people wait until the first day of the year to begin something? Too busy? Not enough money? No matter what you say, it's simply a form of procrastination.

You'll do it later? I doubt it. Did that make you mad when I told you that you would not do it later? Do you know why it makes us angry? Because you now know what it takes to act in leadership. You know the first step to getting healthier: to do what those who live in the blue zones do, yet you did not or will not act on it. This lack of alignment between knowing and acting on that knowledge is called cognitive dissonance.

> Cognitive dissonance; *the state of having inconsistent thoughts, beliefs, or attitudes, especially as relating to behavioral decisions and attitude changes.*

When we do not act in accordance with what we know to be the right path, it causes anxiety and stress, often triggering anger toward anyone who points it out.

I'm not a psychologist, but one does not need a PhD. to understand basic human behavior. Remember the four types of suffering outlined in Buddhism.

- Dukka – Life contains suffering. Some unavoidable, some self-inflicted.
- Samudaya – The origins of the self-inflicted suffering.
- Nirodha – The solution is to remove the self-inflicted suffering.
- Magga – The path to removing the self-inflicted suffering.

We know the origin of the self-inflicted suffering, knowledge of the solution, and the action to accomplish removing it. You did it to yourself, and it's avoidable. Did you need some elaborate goals to get started in removing unhealthy foods from your home? No, you didn't. Most things do not require some elaborate goal-setting plan. Perhaps that is why you did not get started. Let me help you with that by gaining insight into how some goal-setting strategies can be in direct contrast to acting in leadership.

Goal Setting Gone Wrong

Have you read any books on goal setting? Let me tell you the downfalls with most of what is taught.

The S.M.A.R.T. acronym first appeared in the November 1981 issue of Management Review. The article "There's a S.M.A.R.T. way to write management goals and objectives" was written by George Doran, Arthur Miller, and James Cunningham. Here are the original labels of the acronym.

S – Specific, M – Measurable, A – Assignable,
R – Realistic, and T – Time-Related

If you've ever read Duran, Miller, and Cunningham's actual document, the details of their paper provide a fair amount of insight into the proper use of goal setting and its limitations. They tell us that not all objectives at all levels can be or must be quantified. Wait! What the *bleep*? Why haven't I heard this before?

It's a business article written for business by people who have some understanding of business as a whole. We took the general premise of an approach to business and have been applying it to all aspects of our lives. We shouldn't be.

Ok, you love your spouse, kids, other family members, or friends, right? Measure that for us. How much do you love that person? Wait! You don't have a love goal? Why not? Because you don't need one.

The SMART goals platform represents scientific measuring. In 1911, Frederick Winslow Taylor published his book *The Principles of Scientific Management*. Taylor is responsible for advancing automation and scientific measurement in the industrial world. Ford's mass production of the automobile resulted from implementing Taylor's principles. The best part is that Taylor provides us with the massive benefits of measuring things in the industrial world, but it's not the *first thing* he talks about in his book. People skipped over the other things he taught, just like people left out many of the details of the original paper for effective use of SMART goals.

Fast-forward to 1981, and people have used the SMART goals platform to implement scientism into all aspects of life, when it is meant for some aspects of business. Scientism is the excessive belief in the power of scientific knowledge and techniques.

Scientism implies that scientific measuring is the only way to determine when a progression happens. It's not. A good thinker recognizes that science is one way, but it's not the only way.

At a minimum, a business must sell enough of its products or services to pay all the expenses to stay operating. If that is not accomplished, the company will cease to exist. Therefore, a specific revenue goal is set, then broken into bite-sized pieces, daily, weekly, monthly, quarterly, and annually, as a method to stay on track. That's necessary in business. That same strategy is unnecessary in order to progress toward a healthier you. Using that same strategy has so many negative factors it flies in the face of acting in leadership.

Let's say you want to begin acting in leadership by exercising. What's your plan? What's your goal? Where do you start? Here's what you shouldn't do—something like setting a goal of losing thirty pounds in thirty days and then attempting to create some elaborate plan to accomplish it. Numeric goals, when done wrong, can mislead us. Remember Goodhart's Law and Ethical Fading from chapter 23? "When a measure becomes a target, it ceases to be a good measure."

When you combine resistance training with any variation of exercise designed to lose weight, you will add muscle mass. Muscle has weight. In fact, it is denser than fat and takes up less space in our bodies. If you lose 10 pounds of fat and add six pounds of muscle, your fat loss appears to be four pounds. You lost ten pounds of fat, but the scale tells you something else.

That's just one example of how incorrect goal setting using scientific measuring will lead a person astray. If the primary indicator is not measuring your weight, what do you do? We go back to the basics of understanding the purpose of goals.

Goals help us indicate what is important, determine where to focus our time and efforts and consider what must be traded off to progress naturally.

Goals help us to indicate what is important. Goals help us determine where to focus our time and efforts, including what must be traded off to progress naturally. ~Scott M. Carter

Let me repeat that. Goals help us to determine what is important to us. Identifying what is important does not require a numerical value.

If your goals are too specific, too many, or too challenging, your chances of continuing to progress toward a goal will significantly diminish. We've escalated to putting "stretch goals" into the mix, which have serious side effects.

If setting a specific, too-challenging of a goal isn't the strategy, then how does a person proceed? You measure the consistency of your daily actions toward getting healthy. You do not measure by comparing your progress to an arbitrary weight loss goal or by comparing yourself to others or what others do.

Track what you do each day in some journal, either a physical journal or one in the digital world. What did you do today? Then, after thirty days, look back and see how many times you exercised. The same goes for your eating habits. Write down what you eat each day and when. Then, look back to see how you did.

Do you know the purpose of a control group? Control groups serve as vital benchmarks against which to compare the experimental group's results. It's how you measure progress. When it comes to your health, what are you measuring against? Other people? Why? What is the best control group for you? *You!* You are the only proper control group against which to compare yourself.

Comparing ourselves to others can trigger a cycle of stress and anxiety. Constantly striving to meet unrealistic standards set by others can lead to chronic stress, as we feel pressured to achieve what others have achieved.

These triggered cycles are all scientifically proven when it comes to unhealthy comparisons. I'm not writing a health and exercise book. I'm illustrating how we get things wrong when it comes to acting in leadership and goal setting. Not all things should or can be measured. When measuring can be and should be done, in most cases, we're measuring the wrong things.

Remember from chapter nineteen, James Clear's *Atomic Habits*? Habit formation has four very simple components.

- Que
- Craving
- Response
- Reward

Why did I tell you to remove all the unhealthy food from your house? Having them there creates a que; you see them. Your brain tells you, "Yummy." Your response is to grab some and eat it. The reward is the fabulous taste. Why are you making some elaborate health plan, which includes arbitrary goals, which in turn cause stress and anxiety, when you haven't built the habit of not having junk food in the house?

James Clears says, "The goal isn't the hard part. The hard part is building a system of behaviors and habits that carry you almost inevitably toward that outcome."

Everyone has missed how both books by Charles Duhigg and James Clear showed us the path to goal setting as well as an intuitive understanding of how our habits determine the trajectory of our lives. Clear puts it this way.

> *One pushup does not transform your body, but it does cast a vote for 'I'm the type of person who doesn't miss workouts.'* ~James Clear

Get down on the floor and do ten pushups today. Then again tomorrow. Pick your level. Do five if you need to. Do not overdo it by going for a hundred because some moron told you, "No Pain, No Gain." If you need to do them on your knees, rather than fully stretched out on your toes, then start there.

Write down what you did and when you did it. You're tracking the building of your habits to become consistent with what it takes to get healthy.

Writing one sentence may not finish the book, but it does cast a vote for "I'm a writer." That was how I began. Now, you are reading my third book in a series of at least five books. I never set a goal of writing five books. Heck, not even two books. What did I do? A little research every day, and a little writing every day. I created a habit; now, writing has become part of my life. You need to make healthy eating and getting moderate exercise part of your life. It will begin to feel out of place when you *do not* do the things that make you healthier.

It took seven years from when I began writing books to when this book was published. The problem is that most people want to have a book like this in seven weeks or seven months, not seven years.

Instead of starting at the beginning by creating the basic habits, what do most people do? They haven't worked out a lick in years, or in some cases, ever. They listen to some so-called expert, and they create some elaborate workout and nutrition plan, set a health goal of some sort, say, lose 30 pounds in thirty days, and then it all falls apart.

> *Excellence is not about making radical changes, but about accruing small improvements over time.* ~James Clear

Removing all the bad food from your house and replacing it with healthier items is not a radical change. The expectations of things like "lose 30 pounds in 30 days" are too daunting for most people. That's a radical change.

In an interview with Joe Rogan, Jordan Peterson, a well-known Canadian psychologist and author, says, "If you aim low enough, you will succeed." This might seem odd to most people, but psychology papers all over the place tell us that we tend to set bars so high that 99% of the time, the goal is impossible to attain. And it does not take much to reach the point of "setting bars too high."

> *If you aim low enough, you will succeed.* ~Jordan Peterson

I bet you weren't expecting some "aim low" advice in a book teaching people how to act in leadership. Surprise!

People consider the little things that lead to big things as trivial. The most critical actions are things we can and should do that will lead to actual improvement. We end up in the mindset, with the belief that we are lowering ourselves to unworthy levels of effort. Some idiot told you it's about the "extra" in extraordinary—another fallacy. If everyone suddenly becomes extraordinary, then by default, everyone is the same, meaning extraordinary becomes commonplace or ordinary.

Peterson says, "You won't lower yourself enough to take the opportunity." We've been brainwashed into some misguided world where the focus is on big things. "This doesn't mean don't aim for something, and it doesn't mean don't aim upward," Says Jordan. There's no glory in the little steps along the way, so people do not do them. Worthy ideals are comprised of little steps.

Combine the misinformation we get about goals with the unpredictability of life, day by day, week by week, year by year, even hour by hour, and we have a recipe for most people not acting in leadership—or at the very least, not acting in leadership consistently and not for longer periods of time.

Life has too many uncertainties. It's unpredictable. It does not repeat in the exact same pattern. It's a Penrose tiling system of non-repeating patterns. Life bounces us around from component to component, the Wonkavator random movements in the BASIC Leadership outer ring.

How do we know what I told you is accurate and part of acting in leadership? It's been known for thousands of years.

Little Leads To Big

> For whoever has will be given more, and they will have an abundance. Whoever does not have, even what they have will be taken from them.
> ~Matthew 25:29 (NIV)[1]

People get things wrong all the time, and I probably did in this book. That quote by Matthew, one of Jesus' twelve disciples, is known as the "Matthew Principle." Sadly, people only equate it to economics and say, "The rich get richer, and the poor get poorer." That's an incorrect analogy.

This passage means that those who act in leadership will reap the benefits, and those who do not, will suffer the consequences of not acting in leadership.

When people make a daily effort to get healthier, they progress and gain more health. If people do not do as those in the blue zones do, moderate, consistent exercise and healthier eating, then their bodies will be diminished in many capacities. What they have, which is their current health, will be taken from them.

Right now, you have a certain level of health. Do nothing to preserve or improve that, and it will be taken from you. People who eat crappy and do not exercise are more susceptible to diseases. Do what it takes to become healthier, and a healthier you will be given to you. Jesus taught acting in leadership. Some higher power isn't doing it to you. And some higher power isn't going to do it *for you.* It's up to you. We saw this same principle in an earlier Greek quote in chapter twenty-nine.

> *Prayer indeed is good, but while calling on the gods a man should lend a hand himself.* ~Hippocrates

What does Buddhism tell us? The small things matter most. We should pay attention to minor daily activities and challenges. Instead, we set unrealistic, arbitrary goals with arbitrary timelines, then hit some perceived wall of non-progress, and we give up.

> *Make the small big and the few many.*
> *Return animosity with virtue.*
> *Meet the difficult while it is easy.*
> *Meet the big while it is small.*
>
> *The most difficult in the world*
> *Must be easy in its beginning.*
> *The biggest in the world*
> *Is small in the beginning.*
> *So, the sage never strives for greatness,*
> *And can therefore accomplish greatness.*
>   ~Lao Tzu, *Tao Te Ching*[2]

This Taoist lesson covers two aspects of acting in leadership. First, these verses tell us we should take care of what might become difficult when it is still easier to deal with right now. Developing healthy habits early in life when a person is young is easier than after a person becomes obese or inflicted by some other condition of not doing what it takes to get and remain as healthy as possible.

A person who is careless about things when they are easy to deal with will have to face them when they become difficult. If a person is somewhat healthy now but fails to do the little things to stay healthy and to become healthier, they will have to face being very unhealthy later in life when it will be more difficult to deal with, both physically and mentally.

You can approach life with virtue, high moral standards regarding your health, or with animosity, which is anger and resentment, blaming others, or something else. You get to choose.

Second, the lesson in this verse of the *Tao Te Ching* also enlightens us about how good things accumulate. Little by little, they become bigger and bigger. That's how trees grow. It's how water carves into rock and creates things like the Grand Canyon. An intelligent and wise person attends to things when they are not difficult.

One of the best books I've ever read, *The Slight Edge* by Jeff Olson, published in 2005, explains this concept in the simplest ways. We often see words like "difficult" used in the lessons we teach. The fact is, nothing is hard or difficult.

> *Making the right choices, taking the right actions. It's truly easy to do. Ridiculously easy. But it's just as easy not to do.* ~Jeff Olson

It's time, effort, and trade-offs. We don't do the little easy things because it's easier not to do them. Both doing and not doing them are easy; not doing them is just easier, so we call the less easy one "difficult." That's a fallacy, a false mindset that causes us never to begin. What does the *Dhammapada* tell us?

> *By oneself evil is done; by oneself one is injured. Do not do evil and suffering will not come.*
>   ~Buddha, *The* Dhammapada[3]

> *Now is the time to wake up, when you are young and strong. Those who wait and waver, with a weak will and a divided mind, will never find the way to pure freedom.*
>   ~Buddha, The Dhammapada[4]

> *Do not fail to do what ought to be done, and do not do what ought not to be done. Otherwise your burden of suffering will grow heavier.*
>   ~Buddha, The Dhammapada[5]

We think of evil as relating only to some God versus Devil concept. Evil refers to doing what we know is not in alignment with integrity and landing on the positive side of the leadership lifeline. Acting without integrity and acting on the negative side of the leadership lifeline is bad, aka evil. Evil means not good. It's the yin-yang principle. Yin is the negative; yang is the positive.

If someone harmed you, you might say they are evil. But what about when you harm yourself, even if it's in tiny increments? Little by little, you make yourself unhealthy. There is no higher level of evil because it is done to you by yourself.

> *He who adds to what he has, will keep off bright-eyed hunger; for it you add only a little to a little and do this often, soon that little will become great.* ~Hesiod[6]

Hesiod was a Greek poet who lived over 200 years before Socrates, Plato, and Aristotle, illustrating how these leadership principles have been understood even longer than we might imagine.

This bears repeating. If you want to avoid bigger, more challenging problems later in life, that is accomplished by doing the little daily things right now that land on the positive side of the leadership lifeline.

It's twofold. Big problems start as small problems and big accomplishments begin with little accomplishments. Doing the little things, at this exact moment, that we think do not matter is *acting in leadership.*

We see other people with great physiques and lots of muscle working out in the gym, and we think that is our goal. That's not how they attained what they have. They didn't walk into the gym and start bench pressing 400 pounds or leap right into a one-hour cycling power class. They started where they could start and progressed to that level through consistency.

We think they live on kale, never eat sweets, and constantly munch on rabbit food. We resort to drastic measures after we have failed to do the little things that matter daily. I'm in great shape at the age of 62 while writing this book. I eat a variety of things, some of which would fall on the negative side of the leadership lifeline in terms of nutrition. That's called moderation. "Nothing to excess" is one of the Greek maxims. Nothing to excess is also applied to the things on the positive side of the leadership lifeline. Excess on the negative side of the leadership lifeline is called escalation. Bodybuilders escalate. I know it. I did it for years.

Remember from chapter twenty-three, Aristotle's list of virtues and their extremes helps us understand moderation and escalation.

Too Little	Balance	Too Much
cowardice	courage	rashness
sloth	ambition	greed

See how easy this is? Life can get complicated quite easily. Sometimes, all we need to do is get back to the basics. Otherwise, we begin to feel overwhelmed.

Taoism, Buddhism, Greek Philosophy, and the *Bible* teach us how to manage actions, relationships, and self-worth—setting big arbitrary goals that are difficult to achieve impacts our self-worth when, over ninety percent of the time, we can't achieve them. People are feeding you wrong information about goal setting. Propaganda under the label of marketing is mainly equated with doing business. They may as well say, "Buy my escalation plan. Most of you will fail."

I used the concept of physical health to make my points about goal setting. It's easy for most of us to grasp. Goal setting for acting in leadership is about the little things that lead to big things and does not require some large, detailed plan. The concepts covered in this chapter apply to every part of our lives. It works the same way with finances as it does with health. Let's look at that next.

CHAPTER THIRTY-THREE

BASIC™ Finances - Acting
In Leadership

We are constantly propagandized not to act in leadership. Why? No one teaches us leadership lessons.

> *A man made a wooden image of Mercury and presented it for sale in the market. As no one offered to buy it, however, he thought he would try to attract a purchaser by proclaiming the virtues of the image. So he cried up and down the market, "A God for sale! A God for sale! One who will bring you luck and keep you lucky." Presently one of the bystanders stopped him and said, "If your God is all you make him out to be, how is it you don't keep him and make the most of him yourself?" "I'll tell you why," replied he. "He brings gain, it is true, but he takes his time about it; whereas I want money at once."* ~Aesop, The Image Seller[1]

I'm laughing because not more than a few days ago, I heard an advertisement offering the perfect system to become wealthy by flipping houses. If the system is so good, why aren't you doing it yourself? If a whole bunch of people all buy your system and begin doing it, won't the market be flooded with people now competing against you, making it harder for you to be successful yourself?

So why sell the system instead of flipping houses yourself? Because it's hard work, takes a long time, and for most people, it has a low probability of actually making money, let alone accumulating wealth. In fact, it is high risk. This image seller gets your money at once.

A slave boy who lived thousands of years ago warned us about how people influence us to part with our money with misleading promises that will fulfill our material desires. Somehow, we think this lesson is new.

If we took all the money in the United States and divided it evenly between everyone, within a very short period of time, most of the same people who originally had most of the money would have it again. Even if a completely different group ended up with most of the money, the point is that the financial dynamics of a society will end up right back where they were before the redistribution. The percentage of people who struggled financially before the distribution would return to that same percentage. If you are struggling now, it would not be long before you would be struggling again.

Redistribution of money is like moving to a Blue Zone to solve your health issues. If you moved to a blue zone, you'd have to change. If you suddenly had lots of money, you would not instantly change your habits. You wouldn't go to a health club four or five days a week. You'd become more of what you already are. That's a fact based on psychological research. For things to change, you must change.

For things to change, you have to change. ~Jim Rohn

Most people want their circumstances to change. "Give me the money, and I'll show you how responsible I am with money. Give me the time, and I'll show you how dedicated I am to getting healthier." Your circumstances do not have to change; *you must.* You haven't built the habits to have more money, to be debt-free, or to be healthier. The "habits" I'm referring to are the small daily habits.

> *Be the change that you wish to see in the world.* ~Mahatma Gandhi

> *All the effort must be made by you; Buddhas only show the way. Follow this path and practice meditation; go beyond the power of Mara.*
>   ~Buddha, *The Dhammapada*[2]

Gandhi said it is you that has to change. If you want the world to change, it starts with you, not someone else. Buddha tells us the same thing about starting with ourselves, how it's a progression, and how practice builds habits.

Like Matthew's earlier quote tells us, you lose good when evil takes over. In the above quote, "Mara" means evil. What you have will be taken. The good will be taken and replaced by evil. And in either case, it happens slowly over time through little increments in one direction or another. Are you seeing the pattern here?

Aristotle's list of virtues and their extremes tells us that sloth, being lazy, is too little. Greed, which is escalation, is too much, but ambition is ok. We escalate the concept of ambition. It's ok to have ambition, an earnest desire for some achievement, as long as it is not for power, honor, fame, wealth, or to outdo someone else, to try to mirror what they achieved.

> *It's ok to have ambition, an earnest desire for some achievement, as long as it is not for power, honor, fame, wealth, or to outdo someone else, to try to mirror what they achieved.* ~Scott M. Carter

Go ahead and try to be the next Michael Jordan, Elon Musk, Oprah Winfrey, or Mary Lou Retton, but most of what is taught about becoming those people is not acting in leadership; it's escalation.

How much money you have does not define who you are. It's a misguided belief that those with lots of money have it because they acted in leadership. Conversely, you cannot change your financial situation without living within the five components that make up the outer ring of the BASIC Leadership blueprint.

If you want to change your financial situation, be careful who you listen to. If someone tells you to set the goal of accumulating a million dollars, and that's the first thing out of their yapper, walk away. Run from them. It's the same premise of losing thirty pounds in thirty days. By the way, I have a house-flipping program you can buy today. Not sure? Wait! I'll throw in some free stuff!

You can't even stop spending an outrageous amount of money on coffee each morning when you're living paycheck to paycheck, and your goal is to accumulate a million dollars? It's like saying you're going to become an astrophysicist but spend your days reading *People* magazine instead of understanding the universe and applying the laws of physics to it.

It's like writing up an elaborate plan for getting in shape without building the habit of showing up at the gym five days a week.

Financial Peace

Dave Ramsey kicked off Financial Peace University in 1994 with a nine-lesson video. Managing money and personal finances wasn't new then, and the fundamental lessons are still the same.

When it comes to acting in leadership, the "peace" aspect is the most important. Why do you suppose Dave Ramsey used that word in the program name? It could have been any name with finances in it. It's about peace of mind. Accumulating financial wealth is not the primary focus. It can be a result. Reducing or eliminating stress and anxiety is the primary focus, hence the word "peace."

Having substantial amounts of debt causes stress and anxiety. Remember from chapter ten, *Nature's Pharmacy*, when you and I are stressed or anxious, Nature punishes us. Both adrenaline and cortisol are released into our bodies. It doesn't kill us instantly. It damages our bodies a little bit at a time. It's like running river water. It starts small, then if small or large amounts over a long period of time run through it, you end up with the Grand Canyon – a gorge over a mile deep.

That's our bodies, adrenaline, and cortisol coursing through our veins, damaging our internal physical landscape. How much stress do you suppose is created when you begin with the goal of accumulating a million dollars and then setting a timeline?

We find ourselves coming full circle back to Dr. Eliot, the Chief of Cardiology at the University of Nebraska, who went on to create the Institute of Stress Medicine in Denver, Colorado. Like many of us, Dr. Eliot appeared healthy and showed no signs of having heart issues. Then *bang*, down he went.

Dr. Eliot provides the science behind the philosophy. The concept of being at peace in our lives has been around for a long time. We'll start with Jesus from the *Bible*. Whether you are religious or not is irrelevant. Pay attention to the lesson being taught here. Jesus is called the Prince of Peace.

> *For a child will be born to us, a son will be given to us; and the government will rest on His shoulders; and His name will be called Wonderful Counselor, Mighty God, Eternal Father, Prince of Peace.* Isaiah 9:6 (NIV)[3]

That translation comes from the Hebrew quote by Isaiah. The full name of this child is "Pele-yoetz-el-gibbor-Abi-ad-sar-shalom." His name is "wonderful counselor-mighty God – Prince of peace." The Hebrew phrase "Shar Shalom" translates to "Prince of Peace." It means "the one who removes all peace-disturbing factors and secures the peace."

Many thought that Jesus would be some warrior who would eliminate their enemies through battles and wars, bringing peace to the world. That wasn't why he existed. He taught leadership, and one of the primary aspects of acting in leadership shows us how to achieve peace of mind. To be content right now, in this moment.

Can you be at peace if you determine your success by comparing yourself to others in terms of wealth and material possessions? The answer is no. You know that because you have common sense. Can you be at peace if you are physically unhealthy and have the knowledge, capacity, and ability to change it? The answer is no.

Peace comes at a price. The good news is that the price is small and easy to pay. It's not even a price to pay. It's what? We covered it. Come on, you can get there. The answer is; trade-offs.

That price to pay is time, effort, and trade-offs. We covered this in chapter fifteen. We get to decide where we spend our time and effort. It takes time and effort to save money and not accumulate debt. It also takes time and effort to spend money and accumulate debt. The concept of time and effort isn't rocket science.

Along with the time and effort, there is always a trade-off. We get to decide what that trade-off is and when it happens. When we choose to accumulate debt now and for the rest of our lives, the trade-off comes later in the form of disease, perhaps cancer, or some other ailment perpetuated by stress chemicals released into our bodies. The slow river waters dig a gorge of damage within our bodies and our financial status. The reason we go into debt? Immediate gratification.

For some reason, people have latched onto many misguided philosophies being taught. I mentioned "Extraordinary" as one misguided philosophy. "Leaders do extraordinary things," they expound. *No, they do not.* Acting in leadership is about doing ordinary things repeated over time.

There's nothing extraordinary about eating healthier every day, working out regularly, saying "no" to impulse buying, or reading ten pages of a book a day. These are the habits that Charles Duhigg talks about in his book, *The Power of Habit.*

> *Champions don't do extraordinary things. They do ordinary things.* ~Tony Dungy

Here's the catch. All the things that land on the positive side of the leadership lifeline are ordinary. All the things that land on the negative side of the leadership lifeline are also ordinary. The habits that determine the trajectory of our lives, good or bad, are ordinary. The criminal in prison or the inventor who ended up a billionaire are both situations due to ordinary habits done consistently over time.

> *Leadership is about doing ordinary things with integrity, on the positive side of the leadership lifeline, consistently over an extended period of time.* ~Scott M. Carter

Be ordinary and do it well. You could be the next great something simply by acting in leadership. And by *the next great something,* I mean the best possible version of you. The next great dad, mom, son, daughter, neighbor, coworker, friend, and so on.

The lessons about small, ordinary actions leading to big things and the lessons about not getting attached to material possessions do not imply that we do nothing at all. Aristotle showed us that there is a middle ground. Earnest ambition in life is necessary to exist.

Too Little	Balance	Too Much
sloth	ambition	greed

Loa Tzu talks about desire but does not imply that every level of desire is bad or an issue.

There is no greater crime than desire.
There is no greater disaster than discontent.
There is no greater misfortune than greed.
Therefore:
To have enough of enough is always enough.
　　　~Lao Tzu, *Tao Te Ching*[4]

Desire is not a crime, but it leads to crime when we covet what others have. Envy exists in this same realm. When we rely on material possessions for happiness, it leads to discontentment. Be content, at peace, now, with what you have, not through desire for something in the future. Nothing in this lesson implies that we cannot organically accumulate things through a natural progression.

> *Don't get selfishly attached to anything, for trying to hold on to it will bring you pain. When you have neither likes nor dislikes, you will be free.*
>
> *Selfish attachment brings suffering: selfish attachment brings fear. Be detached, and you will be free from suffering and fear.*
> ~Buddha, *The Dhammapada*[5]

In short, Buddha tells us attachment is one of the roots of suffering. We fear losing things when we should not. Then suddenly, we learn that fear is false when we lose someone we love, and we'd trade all we have to get them back. Those material possessions we once feared losing hold no value and have no fear of loss attached. Again, none of this implies we do nothing.

> *Better fearless poverty than wealth with its needs and worries.*
> ~Aesop, The Fir Tree and the Bramble Bush[6]

I love Aesop's fables. The fir tree brags about how it will be used to build so many things. It's big and important. That is until the bramble bush reminds the fir tree that in order to do so, it will be cut down painfully with a sharp axe.

None of those quotes, the philosophies of Lao Tzu, Buddha, Greek philosophies, or the *Bible* imply that we should not progress toward goals. In fact, if you earn a living, live well within your financial means, and save a little bit each week, it is impossible not to accumulate money at some level. The difference? You live without the stress, anxiety, and all the other things that come with escalation, comparison to others, and fear of loss.

You've been told that if you do not save X dollars by the time you are XX years of age, you've done life wrong. What a bunch of crap; all propaganda.

I've talked about my friend John Allan in my previous books. John was my close friend and workout partner at our local health club. He grew up practicing martial arts. In his late forties, he could still do both side and front splits all the way to the floor. No matter where we went, it seemed John knew someone, and the interaction with those people was always positive.

One weekend, John and I embarked on one of our canoe trips down the St. Croix River. We launched at noon on a Friday and were hours down the river in the middle of nowhere when we heard a shout from the river bank. Those people recognized John and yelled out to us. They were not close friends who saw John every day; they were people who had encountered John years ago. He helped them out at one point in their lives. No matter where I went with John, I could tell you story after story of this happening.

John was an iron worker his entire career. He lived a modest and simple life in a small house, cutting his own wood to heat it. John had no fancy cars or personal belongings. He had average stuff, but was rich beyond most people's wildest dreams.

I know where your mind went. I know because I see the same ads for how to become a millionaire by the age of XX. John was not a millionaire, yet he left his ironworker job long before the age when most people will leave the workforce. He did so by saving a little over a long period, not accumulating debt or fancy expensive things.

He always wore a smile and was kind and helpful. He was grateful for what he had and did not focus on what he did not have, which is what most people do. John lived a life full of contentment. Through his martial arts training, John learned and practiced the lessons of acting in leadership that were taught thousands of years ago.

John is a shining example of what we could all be. John acted with integrity and on the positive side of the leadership lifeline more often than not. John was more at peace in life than anyone I ever knew.

Remember what we're talking about here. Financial peace is one part of having peace of mind and being content in life. Health, finances, relationships—it's all tied together. We escalate everything looking to achieve what John had his entire life: contentment in the now.

Most people escalate because we've been propagandized to do so. Your best wealth? Your peace of mind. No one can take it from you.

Sadly, we lost John in a road accident in 2014 at the age of 57. John was at peace with his health, finances, and how he lived his life. It was John's mindset that created his life of contentment.

Let's test your beliefs, your mindset.

You're driving along a two-lane road, approaching a traffic light. The light turns red, and you roll to a stop. You look to your left and see a motorcycle pulling up alongside you. The man is wearing what one might consider typical Harley-biker apparel: black boots, jeans, leather chaps, no shirt, and a leather vest with a large patch on the back that represents a motorcycle club. His arms are very muscular, and he has a bandana tied around his head.

What is your first thought?

You just met John, my friend, a motorcycle enthusiast who participated in fundraising for sick children. The large club emblem on his vest? A charity club.

People will read books about greatness, about so-called great people who did extraordinary things and who would be called leaders. That was John – a great man who exemplified acting in leadership.

To my friend John. I miss you, buddy.

Your friend,

Scott

CHAPTER THIRTY-FOUR

Power of the Mind - Part One

According to the Pew Research Center, if you live in the United States, Canada, Australia, Germany, or Finland, you live in the top 7% of the world's wealth. Let me state it another way: If you are among the poorest people in the United States, you live in a country with more abundance than 93% of the world.

Do you know the definition of bountiful? It means to have things in abundance. Abundance is having things in a very large quantity. In many countries, including the United States, people live in a society of abundance.

You can go into any town or city in the United States and get just about anything you want. Not just what we need, the necessities, but anything you want. Sure, that requires money, but we live in a nation where things exist in abundance.

Now, if material things, things that are luxuries, not necessities, are available in abundance and exist in massive quantities, and having those things is supposed to lead to happiness, then why isn't the United States full of the happiest people in the world? How is this possible? Why is there no abundance of peace of mind and contentment? Why is there no abundance of kindness toward one another?

The poorest of the poor, those considered to live in poverty in the United States, have cell phones, large-screen TVs, and convenience stores on every dang corner, yet contentment seems to be a scarcity. How can this be?

Do not point me to the homeless guy or gal. I will call you out on that all day long. We have such an abundance that every single one of those people could be taken care of if we chose to as a society. We could easily feed every hungry child in our entire nation again if we chose to.

Now, I'll ask the same question more definitively. For every person who is not homeless, not lacking food in such a manner as actually to be starving, that means the rest of us, why is contentment such a scarcity? How can this be?

Because contentment is a mindset.

The Power of the Mind

If you knew you could not fail, what would you attempt? Most people would write a fairly long list of things they would attempt.

On May 6, 1954, Roger Bannister became the first person to run a four-minute mile. It did not take long before someone else achieved that same milestone. In June that same year, John Landy ran an even faster mile. In the four years following Bannister's achievement, twenty more people would run a mile in under four minutes. Since then, over 1,600 people have done so.

This story isn't about Bannister himself or how many people can run a four-minute mile. It's about "The Bannister Effect," which refers to the shift in other people's beliefs when they see someone else accomplish something previously thought impossible. Our minds contain the greatest power. Our physical bodies come in a distant second. The body follows the mind.

Jason McElwain was born on October 20, 1988. He did not speak for the first five years of his life and had difficulty chewing solid foods for just as long. Jason has autism.

Eighteen years after his birth, on February 15, 2006, with four minutes and nineteen seconds left in a high school basketball division title game, the coach of the Greece Athena High School Trojans put Jason into the game.

The coach, Jim Johnson, did not do this for publicity or as part of some diversity and inclusivity program. The Trojans had a significant lead over the opposing team, Spencerport High School. This point spread was an opportunity for Jason to play without putting the title in jeopardy.

Jason loved basketball. He had been appointed the team manager and did the same workouts and practice as the varsity team members. He even tried out for the varsity team but did not make it. Jason had autism, but he also had skills.

During the game's final minutes, the players on either team did not sit around and let Jason make shots; both teams played like they had been playing the entire time. This matchup was for a division title.

Jason's first two shots? Both unsuccessful. Then he went on to make 20 points, tying the team record for the most three-point shots in one game. A three-point shot is one made from outside of a half-circle line far away from the basket—no easy feat, even when someone is not attempting to block your shot.

There are many lessons hidden inside this fantastic story. When Jason missed his first two shots, his beliefs were not impacted. His mind did not tell him that missing those two shots meant he would miss on the third attempt.

Jason was not playing for fame, money, or recognition. He was simply excited to be playing the game. Are you simply excited about playing in the game of life, or are you seeking fame, recognition, and fortune?

Jason's skills were a progression over a long period of time. He did not even expect to be in the game. His participation with just minutes left in the game was not preplanned. My question to you, the reader, is this... had they been behind, would the coach have put him in?

Think about that for a minute. Putting him in when they were behind could have been the deciding factor in winning. I believe that coach Johnson would not have thought Jason was the solution to winning in a "come from behind" game. That's how life works. Beliefs drive actions.

Like the Roger Bannister story and the Bannister effect, our minds are our most powerful tool. That power can take us in a positive direction or a negative direction. Everyone's actions in Jason McElwain's story are based on their beliefs in that time and place.

Sitting in front of me as I write this chapter is a copy of the original book from 1908, *Thought Vibration*, by William Walker Atkinson. Sitting next to it is a copy of the original version of *Think and Grow Rich* by Napoleon Hill, published in 1937. Both books provide insight into the power of beliefs. I own many books that all prove that same premise about how our beliefs drive our actions.

In chapter twenty-six, we learned of Dr. Bruce Lipton, who wrote *The Biology of Belief: Unleashing the Power of Consciousness, Matter & Miracles*, published in 2005. Lipton's research provides insight into how our subconscious mind operates in the background, secretly controlling ninety-five percent of our thoughts, which drive our actions. Lipton delivers the science behind what Atkinson and Hill tell us about our subconscious mind and beliefs and confirms what Aristotle told people thousands of years ago about the first six years of our lives.

We work on our physical and financial health, but very few people work on their mental health. By mental health, I'm talking about how our subconscious and conscious minds affect our lives—the power of our minds. In chapter thirty-one, I referenced the placebo effect. Our minds contain the greatest power in the world.

As Earl Nightingale tells us in *The Strangest Secret*, the most valuable things we have been given in life, we have been given for free, yet we do not put them to use.

> *The problem is that our mind comes as standard equipment at birth. It's free. And things that are given to us for nothing, we place little value on. Things that we pay money for, we value. The paradox is that exactly the reverse is true.*
>
> *Everything that's really worthwhile in life came to us free — our minds, our souls, our bodies, our hopes, our dreams, our ambitions, our intelligence, our love of family and children and friends and country. All these priceless possessions are free.*
>
> *But the things that cost us money are actually very cheap and can be replaced at any time. A good man can be completely wiped out and make another fortune. He can do that several times. Even if our home burns down, we can rebuild it. But the things we got for nothing, we can never replace.* ~ Earl Nightingale

That part of Nightingale's radio broadcast in 1957 has had the most profound effect on me. Why is it not a priority for every single person on the planet to learn about the power of our minds? Why aren't the principles of how our beliefs work for and against us the *primary* thing we learn during the early part of our education? Why isn't it mandatory?

We have the science. Is it that we still don't believe we can change our brains, and our thoughts, and by doing so, it will change our lives? Now, that's quite the example of irony right there. We believe our beliefs do not matter.

We are the Hologram in the movie, *The Time Machine*. "Practical Application?" we think to ourselves as we scoff at the thought of being able to exercise our minds like we do our physical bodies or affect the balance sheet of our finances. Then, finally, we see that practical application does exist, and it's been around a very long time.

Exercising the mind is just like the body and our finances; a little bit at a time, it leads to big changes.

We talk about the Bannister Effect like this concept is somehow new. It's centuries old, and our beliefs are the foundation for everything we've covered in the previous two chapters about health and finances. We see stories of Jason McElwain and miss most of the life lessons being taught. We miss seeing the John Allan's in our life because of our beliefs—a Harley dude with a patch on his vest. We quietly roll up our car window and try not to make eye contact because we have many misguided beliefs.

Your Mind Controls Your Emotions

Anger and ill will, any type of resentment, are afflictions and diseases. We must look at them as such. They release the internal chemicals that damage our bodies. We learned that too much cortisol and adrenaline are bad news.

If someone told you that resentment and anger release cancer cells, would you find a way to prevent yourself from ever becoming angry? I would hope so.

Your ill will toward someone harms you for sure, but not necessarily the other person. A.A., Alcoholics Anonymous, teaches this lesson in their twelve-step program.

> *I think resentment is when you take the poison and wait for the other person to die.* ~M.T. A Sponsorship Guide for 12-Step Programs (1995)

That quote is often attributed to Saint Augustine, who lived from 354 AD to 430 AD. Guess who inspired Saint Augustine? Socrates, Plato, and Aristotle.

> *Socrates said that envy was the ulcer of the soul.* ~Stobaeus1

Remember from chapter seventeen, Joannes Stobaeus compiled anthologies containing extracts from hundreds of writers, poets, and philosophers.

In the *Bible*, the Apostle Paul writes letters to the Ephesians. Many of those letters enlighten us on some lessons of acting in leadership. Ephesians 4 contains instructions for living a Christian-based life. We see a direct connection to the Alcoholics Anonymous quote, which is not surprising since A.A. is faith-based.

> *Get rid of all bitterness, rage and anger, brawling and slander, along with every form of malice.*
> ~Ephesians 4:31 (NIV)[1]

Aeschylus was a Greek playwright who lived from 524 BC to 455 BC. In one of his plays, *Prometheus Bound*, he says anger is a disease, and words can heal anger. Today, his insights are a reality.

Envy is an ulcer. Anger is a disease. History has warned us about all of the things that release the damaging chemicals into our bodies and slowly kill us. They knew it without all the scientific evidence we have today.

Both John Allan and Jason McElwain lived lives at a higher level without anger and envy than most people. Do you think Jason McElwain would have been angry, envious, or resentful had he not been put into that basketball game? Based on the interviews I've read, I can tell you with a high level of certainty that he would not. And I know with 100% certainty that I never saw John get angry or envious. John chose not to do so. It's a choice. I cannot say the same thing about many of my conscious decisions. Can you?

Thousands of years ago, no one knew about the physically damaging effects of anger on the body, including Aeschylus, who lived prior to Socrates, Plato, and Aristotle. They didn't have the EEG, the electroencephalogram, which records the brain's electrical activity. Dr. Lipton used this device to understand brain activity.

When Rick Hanson, Ph. D., and Richard Mendius, MD, wrote *Buddha's Brain*, published in 2009, they listed 17 pages of resources, consisting of studies and science they referenced to show the impact of training the mind. Buddha taught these lessons thousands of years ago.

> *By oneself is evil done; by oneself one is injured. Do not do evil and suffering will not come.*
> ~Buddha, *The Dhammapada*[3]

We learn other lessons through phrases such as, "Sticks and stones may break my bones, but words will never hurt me." Words from others cannot harm us unless we allow those words to harm us. Things like anger, envy, discontentment, ill will, resentment, revenge, and jealousy are from within ourselves. Those things will absolutely harm us. Ill will towards others and resentment is like drinking poison ourselves and then hoping it harms others.

> *Truly, only those who see illness as illness*
> *Can avoid illness*
> *The Sage is not ill,*
> *Because he sees illness as illness.*
> *Therefore he is not ill.*
> ~Lao Tzu, *Tao Te Ching*[4]

As we learned in chapter twenty-three, Lao Tzu does not discuss illnesses as we think of them, such as the flu or the common cold. He does not imply that anyone who follows the principles of the *Tao Te Ching* will not experience common physical illnesses.

He's referring to how our thoughts, emotions, and actions cause us to be ill. Anger, resentment, envy, and other emotions are types of illness because they damage us. Again, we must view them that way and treat them accordingly.

The Sage, often translated to "leader," does not act in manners that cause harm to himself or herself. It's almost as if Lao Tzu knew that our bodies release damaging chemicals. It wasn't until the early 1900s that we learned of cortisol and adrenaline. Even later, we learned scientifically how stress, anxiety, anger, and other emotions trigger the release of these chemicals.

CHAPTER THIRTY-FIVE

Power of the Mind - Part Two

What have we learned about leadership in its true essence so far? Progressing toward a healthier you is acting in leadership. Progressing toward better financial health is acting in leadership. Both of those things, as well as any other worthy ideals, will be based on your mindset, your beliefs.

Health and finances are just two concepts I used to illustrate what it means to act in leadership. The BASIC Leadership blueprint works for the progression of any worthy ideal: progressing toward peace of mind and contentment, progressing toward being more kind, progressing toward gaining insight on any subject, perhaps speaking a second language. It all starts with beliefs. That is why we have talked a lot about beliefs in this book.

A person can change their physical health and financial situation. By acting in leadership, a person can also reduce stress, anxiety, fear, and worry. The reduction in stress, anxiety, fear, and worry begins in the mind. It's a conscious choice.

A healthier you requires you to stop putting unhealthy things into your body and replace those things with healthier things. Being active, doing resistance and cardiovascular training are the basics of being healthier.

Healthier finances require reducing spending, increasing savings, and perhaps increasing the amount of money coming in. This also requires an ongoing, never-ending financial plan of some kind. That's the basics of being healthier financially.

There is nothing complicated about health or finances in relation to acting in leadership. How do you suppose it might work when it comes to our minds, our thoughts, and our beliefs?

Changes in any part of our lives—health, finances, relationships, pretty much everything—begin with our beliefs. In fact, belief is a component within itself. A person will only change something if they believe that change is possible.

Therefore, our thoughts, which control the direction and the trajectory of our lives, need a process that allows us to be in charge. So, again, how do you suppose it might work regarding our minds, thoughts, and beliefs?

The amount of good input versus bad input we are exposed to in life is way out of balance, including, most importantly, the thoughts in our heads. What we tell ourselves consciously and subconsciously.

The average number of thoughts we can have on any given day is around 6,000 or 6.2 per minute. That's the only real scientific data I found. It comes from a study by Julie Tseng and Jordan Poppenk, "Brain meta-state transitions demarcate thoughts across task contexts exposing the mental noise of trait neuroticism." Welcome to my world of research.

That massive number of 60,000 daily thoughts you see smattered around the internet doesn't make any sense mathematically, nor could I find any actual study to back it up. How do you get inside a person's head to measure it? Julie Tseng and Jordan Poppenk found a way, so we'll use their data.

6,000 is still a crap load of subconscious thoughts popping in and out of our heads. One every ten seconds sounds about right, as I try to concentrate and not let them into my head while I write. Of those thoughts, what do we think the balance of negative versus positive might be?

Negative Bias

We had no idea what negative bias was until recently, at least scientifically. Again, it was known thousands of years ago. Thucydides was an Athenian Historian who lived c.472 to c.396 BC.

> *When a man finds a conclusion agreeable, he accepts it without argument, but when he finds it disagreeable, he will bring against it all the forces of logic and reason.* ~Thucydides

Thucydides is enlightening us on the concept of bias, both negative and positive. Bias is based on what a person believes. We do not like it when our beliefs are challenged, and we will fight to protect those beliefs. We will also align with others who believe what we believe.

When you purchase a vehicle, it seems that suddenly, more people own that same model. We never noticed them before, but now that we have one, we see them all over the place. This can also affirm that others thought owning one was a good choice; therefore, we made a good choice. That is a form of confirmation bias.

One of the most potent forms of bias is negative bias. Bias has been built into our biology over thousands of years. The systems in our bodies have a higher level of response to negative stimuli because we were exposed to threats and adverse conditions in everyday life—the kind of threats and conditions that determine the difference between life and death. The result? The systems in our bodies have a higher level of response to negative stimuli. Our bodies and minds are stimulated more by negative things than positive things.

Psychologists Paul Rozin and Edward Royzman first documented negativity bias in their 2001 paper, "Negativity Bias, Negativity Dominance, and Contagion." The paper hypothesized that humans and animals give higher weight to negative entities, which manifested in four different ways. Adverse events seem dominant as negative entities and are more contagious than positive ones. In short, negativity has been biologically built into us and is contagious.

Turn on your local news. How much of it is positive? One or two feel-good stories and the rest is doom and gloom, the tragedies of the day. Even the weather is sensationalized. Is it 5 degrees here in Minnesota right now? Nope, "it feels like -15." It has to be colder than it actually is, or people won't tune into their station. Everything is sensationalized; that's why I mentioned the 60,000 thoughts per day. Someone had to sensationalize it to get people's attention. Most information we are fed, sensationalized or not, leans toward the negative.

A coworker turns their cell phone toward you, showing you a random video. Most of these are not feel-good; something great happened today videos. It's a gory accident, someone cutting someone off in traffic resulting in a fistfight, or some guy riding his bicycle off the garage roof onto a trampoline. I like to call that "thinning the herd." Weeding out the stupid is a good start, but sadly, they always seem to survive.

Don't get me started on politics. Candidates constantly attempt to sway us for our vote. All parties, and all sides continually battle, tell lies, and pit us against one another. Creating a large government to retain control, protecting the political party and hierarchy at all costs, requires chaos among the masses. That's politics in a nutshell. See how easy it is to be completely negative? I did it right there—a tirade of negativity.

We're drawn to it. We're also drawn to sugar, and we know too much sugar is bad for us. What do we do? We limit the sugar and replace it with healthier stuff. The real danger comes from within, not from outside of ourselves. I watch those same videos when someone shows them to me, and I can assure you that they haven't turned me into Mr. Always Negative, so that's not the real danger.

The critical danger is our thoughts, which we verbalize. Those thoughts then become our reality. So, how should we handle all the negativity that we're consuming that can impact our thoughts? How do we address the negative thoughts that increase our level of stress, anxiety, and fear, which all impact our ability to be content and have peace of mind?

It has two parts. First, we reduce the negativity, and second, replace it with something healthier. It's a nutrition program for our mind. A banking account where we deposit positivity.

I spent time as a corporate sales trainer. A vital training component addressed having the sales teams turn off the news and stop listening to talk radio with any political affiliation. Keep that crap as far from your life as you can. That doesn't mean living in a cave and not being informed, but being aware of how it impacts your attitude.

Reducing our exposure to negative news feeds, videos, talk radio, and any other form that thrives on negativity is a start. We separate from those around us who whine about everything, complain, and talk about how the world is against them. People who constantly do those things are not acting in leadership.

We develop the habit of negative thinking through input. These negative thought habits consist of self-inflicted worry and stress. The four truths presented by Buddha show us how they are self-inflicted: Dukka and Samudaya, the types of suffering and their origins. We do it to ourselves, and we have the methods to counter it, to begin reversing the effects of an onslaught of negativity.

When a person reverses, or at the very least, mitigates all this negativity, they are acting in leadership. Let's not forget the premise of this book, the one you are reading right now. It's how the BASIC Leadership blueprint helps us define when we are acting in leadership.

Along with reducing the negative input, like lowering our sugar intake, we *must* add some good stuff. Our minds, like our physical bodies, require input. Like our finances, stability requires us to make deposits. Deposits into our minds are already being made; we're just not controlling them. How do we control them? Where does the answer exist? It exists in all of the things we have already discussed. A deep and rich history exists that enlightens us on the concept of *Positive Thought*.

Over the centuries and millennia, it has gone by many names. In the late 1800s and early 1900s, those who provided us with the exact blueprint called it the Law of Attraction. That period was the New Thought Movement. Following that period, others like Napolean

Hill called it Autosuggestion. As we progressed into the late 1900s, we saw the label of Affirmations attached to Personal Development. When we go back thousands of years, we see the labels of Meditation and Prayer. In the following chapters, we'll gain some insight into these concepts to understand better the methods for achieving peace of mind, which is associated with reduced stress, anxiety, fear, and worry.

CHAPTER THIRTY-SIX

Meditation, Prayer, and Affirmations

As James Clear tells us in his book *Atomic Habits*, "You do not rise to the level of your goals. You fall to the level of your system."

If physical activity and eating healthy foods in healthy quantities are the take-action systems for a healthier you, and saving a little each week and not accumulating debt are the take-action systems for being financially healthy, then affirmations, prayer, and meditation are the take-action systems for a healthy, calm, and at peace mind.

> *If you meditate earnestly, pure in mind and kind in deeds, leading a disciplined life in harmony with the dharma, you will grow in glory. If you meditate earnestly, through spiritual disciplines you can make an island for yourself that no flood can overwhelm.*

The immature lose their vigilance, but the wise guard it as their greatest treasure. Do not fall into the ways of sloth and lust. Those who meditate earnestly attain the highest happiness.
~Buddha, *The Dhammapada*[1]

According to Buddha, the Dharma teaches us to be disciplined. Disciplined in what? Living with integrity on the positive side of the leadership lifeline. A healthy mind is achieved through progression and a constant journey of reducing anger, hate, greed, envy, vengeance, and worldly desires. A wise person takes this path, and that person guards this as their greatest treasure.

A person must meditate earnestly. Approaching anything "earnestly" means taking it seriously, not lightly, casually, or flippantly. If you want to do well in school, you study earnestly. If you want to be physically healthy, you eat and exercise earnestly.

Living with contentment and peace of mind is the one thing no one can take from you unless you let them. That's what Buddha means when he says, "you can make an island for yourself that no flood can overwhelm."

We also see alignment with Aristotle's list of virtues and their extremes. Don't be lazy like a sloth, and lust are both forms of escalation in opposite directions. We lust after wealth and material possessions. Translations use different words that relay the same message. Lust and greed both fall into the escalation category.

How did Jesus illustrate the concept of praying to his disciples? He taught them the Our Father prayer. If you were asked what the primary purpose of this prayer is, could you explain it? What lessons was Jesus attempting to teach, and for what purpose?

> *Our Father, who art in heaven, hallowed be Thy name; Thy kingdom come; Thy will be done on earth as it is in heaven. Give us this day our daily bread; and forgive us our trespasses as we forgive those who trespass against us; and lead us not into temptation but deliver us from evil.*

We forgive those who trespass against us. What does that mean? It's not a person trespassing on your property. It's about how to deal with any transgression that would cause you to be angry, resentful, hateful, and to seek revenge. Someone stole from you, lied to you, or cut you off in traffic. Someone at work took your idea and presented it as their own.

You end up carrying that resentment and anger around like a marathon runner with a bag of bricks on their back. You forgive that person, not to let them off the hook for their transgression, but to remove the bag of bricks from your back. It's how you achieve peace of mind. Do not live under the heavy weight of those things that fall on the leadership lifeline's negative side.

Lead us not into temptation but deliver us from evil. What does that mean? We know the word evil means things that are bad for us and fall on the negative side of the leadership lifeline. We shouldn't be tempted to seek material things to achieve happiness, to lust after things, or to act greedily.

If the universe or a higher power is pure in its nature, then we should seek to live in the same manner—not to live perfectly but to have a positive life trajectory. The early Greek philosophers understood these same concepts. The following is from Nicomachean Ethics, book five, part one by Aristotle.

Since the unjust man is grasping, he must be concerned with goods-not all goods, but those with which prosperity and adversity have to do, which taken absolutely are always good, but for a particular person are not always good. Now men pray for and pursue these things; but they should not, but should pray that the things that are good absolutely may also be good for them, and should choose the things that are good for them.[2]

In his speech, Aristotle explains how the praying he's referring to removes anger, hate, greed, envy, vengeance, and worldly desires, replacing them with good things. He goes into great detail about how people pray for the wrong things. In other words, they use prayer to ask for material things when they should be focusing on filling their minds with thoughts that lead to removing anger, hate, greed, envy, vengeance, and worldly desires. Where would he get these ideas? We see it all tied together in the 147 Delphi maxims displayed in the temple of Apollo.

Lao Tzu teaches the same thing using maxims. Throughout the *Tao Te Ching*, many verses show us the details, just as the Delphi maxims address the individual parts of the lessons, representing the leaves farther out on the giant oak tree of semantic learning.

Attain utmost emptiness.
Abide in steadfast stillness.
   ~Lao Tzu, *Tao Te Ching*[3]

These verses are about calming our minds. Focusing on positive things creates a stillness. It removes the thoughts of anger, resentfulness, hate, and the desire to seek revenge. It's about a focus on being thankful for what you have now, not a desire for more.

Lao Tzu, Buddha, Jesus, and Greek philosophers provide instruction manuals on creating peace of mind and contentment.

They understood this thousands of years ago. Now we have the science. In chapter thirty-four, we saw a reference to Rick Hanson, PhD., and Richard Mendius, MD, who published their book *Buddha's Brain: The Practical Neuroscience of Happiness, Love, and Wisdom* in 2009.

Their book draws on all the latest research, combining the intersection of psychology, neurology, and contemplative practice. Hanson and Mendius provide the science of the brain as it relates to what all four of these cultures taught. They focus on Buddhism.

As I sit here today writing, I have three books on my desk: *Buddha's Brain* by Hanson and Mendius, *What the Buddha Taught* by Walpola Rahula, and *The Dhammapada* by Eknath Easwaran. One book is a translation of Buddha's teachings, one provides insight into the lessons within the teachings, and the other is the modern science of the effects on our brains based on neurology and physiology.

Just as eating healthy and working out can transform our bodies, prayer, meditation, and affirmations can transform our minds. It's scientifically proven that when a person does them earnestly, they become a habit.

In 2020, Ernst T. Bohlmeijer, Jannis T. Kraiss, Philip Watkins, and Marijke Schotanus-Dijkstra released their paper on gratitude, "Promoting Gratitude as a Resource for Sustainable Mental Health." Here's what they found.

The health benefits of being thankful, grateful, and having gratitude include,

- ✓ Reduced depression, anxiety, and stress.
- ✓ Improved sleep – the ability to get to sleep faster and a more restful sleep
- ✓ Strong social relationships
- ✓ Combats negative thinking patterns
- ✓ Positively affects biomarkers associated with the risk of heart disease.
- ✓ keeping a gratitude journal can cause a significant drop in diastolic blood pressure – the force your heart exerts between beats. Even if you don't write them down, it also helps your heart by slowing and regulating your breathing to synchronize with your heartbeat.

"Holy Benefits Batman," the boy wonder would exclaim if he were here to talk about gratitude.

Let gratitude be the pillow upon which you kneel to say
your nightly prayer. And let faith be the bridge you
build to overcome evil and welcome good.
>~Maya Angelou,
>*Celebrations: Rituals of Peace and Prayer*

Maya Angelou was a civil rights activist. She published seven autobiographies, three essays, and several poetry books and is credited with a list of plays, movies, and television shows spanning over 50 years. She received dozens of awards and more than 50 honorary degrees.

Do not spoil what you have by desiring what you have not; remember that what you now have was once among the things you only hoped for. ~Epicurus

Let us rise up and be thankful, for if we didn't learn a lot today, at least we learned a little. And if we didn't learn a little, at least we didn't get sick. And if we got sick, at least we didn't die; so let us all be thankful. ~Gautama Buddha

Our gratitude and appreciation for what we have right now are diminished or even canceled by our desire for something we do not have. Then, we get the next thing we want, only to desire something else—a vicious cycle that never lets a person have peace of mind.

Epicurus, 341-270 BC., wrote upwards of three hundred books. Epicurus' quote illustrates how the concept has existed for thousands of years. Not only did Buddha enlighten us on gratefulness, but he also showed us how to create a pattern of comparable items.

You see, we seem to easily create excuses in our minds, but we have not been trained on "being grateful" strategies and have not developed the habit of making comparisons that easily allow us to find things to be grateful for.

Do I really need to give you examples of others who are less fortunate than you? If so, then let's go big or go home.

Nick Vujicic is a Christian and an evangelist. He travels and speaks about his testimony of faith in Jesus Christ. His ministry is known as Life Without Limbs. That's right, he was born without arms and legs, yet he created a growing ministry, teaching people the principles taught by Jesus, aka, acting in leadership. You should probably be thankful for your arms and legs. Better yet, you should put yours to use by acting in leadership.

When we avert a disaster or something terrifying, we say things like, "Thank God," even if we also say we do not believe in a higher power. But we do not practice the art of being thankful. What an odd thing. We know we should be, and we pray for help in times of need. Then why not always, since it has so many benefits?

Now, let's bring this full circle. What is the best way to establish a mindset of gratitude? It involves mediation, prayer, and affirmations and has a boatload of scientifically proven benefits.

Meditation, prayer, and affirmations are part of the nutrition program for your brain. Coupled with knowledge, it is a powerful pairing for living a better life.

When it comes to physical health, you include physical activity and proper nutrition. For finances, you save while you avoid accumulating debt. Your mind works the same way. It requires more than just knowledge input, which is all we seem to focus on these days.

Meditation, prayer, and affirmations provide a system for progressing toward the goal of removing anger, hate, greed, envy, vengeance, and worldly desires, leading to peace of mind and contentment, a healthy mind. We want to avoid accumulating anger, hate, greed, envy, vengeance, and worldly desires just like we avoid accumulating body fat and debt.

When you progressively calm your mind and work to retain a certain level of calm and creativity, new ideas and solutions to problems appear at a much higher rate. I bet I can quickly get your attention if you are somewhere at or near the top of a business hierarchy.

You want creativity, new ideas, solutions to problems, and people to innovate, correct? You achieve higher levels of those things when people reduce stress and anxiety, replacing that with a more peaceful mind. A calm and quiet mind is not one devoid of thought. It is quite the opposite.

Do you want everyone in your organization to be creative, provide new ideas, innovate to become more proficient, or just the people at the top? If your answer isn't "everyone," you shouldn't be at the top of any company or corporate hierarchy. You see, acting in leadership does not require a person to be in any position in any hierarchy.

Meditation, prayer, and affirmations provide a system to progress toward removing anger, hate, greed, envy, vengeance, and worldly desires, leading to peace of mind and contentment, as well as a healthy mind.

These mind-calming processes are part of acting in leadership in its true essence. But before you run off and begin to create a calm mind, there's a lot of misinformation about affirmations, prayer, and meditation. I warned you that we are being fed a bunch of doo doo.

Like the sugars and processed carbs that we buy through food propaganda.... oops, marketing strategies telling us we are saving by using coupons, along with others telling us they can provide us with convenience...and, oh yeah, a food pyramid with a purpose other than creating a healthy society, we're also getting fed incorrect information on affirmations, prayer, and meditation.

CHAPTER THIRTY-SEVEN

Misconceptions About Meditation, Prayer, and Affirmations

What we get wrong

We think meditation is about emptying our minds. This is not true. We also think praying is about asking for things. This is also not true. We'll begin with mediation.

Meditation dates back thousands of years. It's a variety of practices that focus on mind-body integration. I'm not sure how that turned into "empty your mind." Your body follows your mind. Beliefs lead to actions, or worse, inaction when action is needed or action when inaction is needed.

Meditation is about directing or redirecting our thoughts, not eliminating them. You can't empty your mind. Remember from the previous chapter we have on average, 6,000 thoughts a day. Do you think you can stop that process? Good luck. It would be like trying to stop a person from dreaming. I dream vividly almost every single night. Here's what I can tell you. The attitude I have each day, plus the input the last hour or so before bedtime, impacts what I dream about. My dreams do not stop, but I can influence the content, and that content comes from my subconscious mind.

Thoughts are things, just like air. Just because we can't see them doesn't mean they don't exist or that we can't direct them. We constantly redirect air in our favor for things like air travel. Mulford got it right when he named his book *Thoughts Are Things* back in 1908. Meditation addresses our thoughts and deals with our conscious and subconscious minds.

Meditation methods include focusing on simple things like breathing, which normally goes unnoticed, listening to a sound, or focusing on a specific positive visual image.

What we accomplish is mindfulness, awareness of our thoughts, the release of good chemicals into our bodies, and peace of mind. Peace of mind means we are not focused on worrying, are not in a state of stress, and are not filled with anxiety and fear. This is not happiness. It is a state of contentment, a settling of the mind. How do misconceptions like emptying our mind arise? Simple. Depending on which book a person reads, the word is in the translation. The first line in chapter sixteen of the *Tao Te Ching* by Lao Tzu can be interpreted as "Empty you mind," or "Attain utmost emptiness."

While the translation may use those words, think of your mind as the cache on your computer. A cache is software used to store temporary data in your computer. You should clear your browser's cache and temporary internet files regularly because it helps your computer or device run optimally.

Lao Tzu is talking about reducing the constant chatter in our heads so we have a clear mind. Like a cache on your computer, the temporary files in your head will fill back up. They need to be cleared regularly. Remember, we're being exposed to propaganda constantly, most of which is negative.

Meditation is not about sitting around all day humming "ohhhhmmm" with your legs crossed and the tips of your fingers pressed together. None of that is required. Who told you that you need to sit like that? Some stoner from the 1960s? A comedy or action film? Oh, wait, an internet influencer sitting on a yoga mat. Yeah, that last one.

You do not need to shave your head, wear a robe, or put flowers in your hair. Pressing your fingers together is a method used to focus your mind. Sitting on a kitchen chair with your back straight and hands on your thighs works just fine. You can do this anywhere, anytime, and multiple times daily.

> *God grant me the serenity to accept the things I cannot change, courage to change the things I can, and the wisdom to know the difference.*

That is the Alcoholics Anonymous version of Reinhold Niebuhr's serenity prayer. These lessons are everywhere. Again, Lao Tzu tells us it's about returning to the source of serenity. Serenity means a state of calmness. Peace of mind means we are not focused on worrying, are not in a state of stress, and are not filled with anxiety, fear, and uncertainty. It can be both about happiness and a state of contentment, a settling of the mind.

When you meditate or pray, focusing on images of the good things in life, which we are surrounded by but choose not to see, you will find yourself smiling while meditating. For example, you achieve a form of happiness just thinking about something like that little giggle of a child when they are playing.

We see how Lao Tzu finishes this lesson by telling us that we can better deal with whatever life throws at us when we are calm. Opportunity mixed with difficulty is life in a nutshell. Life will come at us each and every day. Do you want to approach it in a state of stress and anxiety or a state of calmness?

In the 1980s and 1990s, corporations paid Jim Rohn big bucks to talk with their executives. I love Jim's interviews. When the top executives asked him to help them determine what the next ten years would bring, he replied, " The next ten years will look just like the last ten years. Opportunity mixed with difficulty." I had no idea just how right he was until I dug deep into the history of that statement.

Now that we've cleared up misconceptions about meditation, let's do the same with prayer. We think praying is about asking for stuff. Who started that poo poo? Jesus certainly didn't say or imply that.

It probably comes from passages like Matthew 7:7-8 which contains the word "ask." The Bible does not tell us it is about asking for things. Praying is a form of meditation. It's about creating positivity, calmness, and peace of mind. Remember, from chapter thirty-three, Jesus is known as The Prince of Peace.

> *Ask and it will be given to you; seek and you will find; knock and the door will be opened to you. For everyone who asks receives; the one who seeks finds; and to the one who knocks, the door will be opened.* ~Matthew 7:7-8 (NIV)[1]

Prayer is not about simply getting our way or about getting things. This is one of the most misunderstood passages in the *Bible*. Jesus talked a lot about a power greater than ourselves, and getting to heaven. Here is my question to you. In all the lessons that Jesus taught his disciples, have you seen any lessons about accumulating material things, or achieving a status in a hierarchy? The answer is "no."

If the answer is no, then what does the first line in Matthew 7:7-8 mean? What are we asking to be given? What are we seeking? Why are we knocking on a door that we want opened, and for what purpose?

Jesus constantly presented lessons to his disciples. Many of the current-day lessons for acting in leadership were created from those lessons, and many of them are about our beliefs, how we think, our attitude, and our mindset.

Jesus promises peace of mind, not material things or status. The "ask" in this Bible quote refers to the method for achieving peace of mind and contentment. You have to want it. You have to ask yourself and give yourself permission for it. Opening the door and getting those things is done through prayer, meditation, and the use of affirmations.

You knock on the door of your own thoughts, and it opens for you to enter. The door is open for contentment and calm in your life. Could it mean more? Could it be more? Sure, as all things can. In religion, many say it is about getting closer to God. That is done by acting as Jesus did. Jesus taught acting in leadership.

We are working on the basics of acting in leadership. The one who seeks finds. Finds what? It could be many things, but the basics, where we need to start, are controlling our thoughts. You find peace of mind when you knock, and the door opens so you can proactively control what goes into your mind.

People want to jump right to asking for the healing of others when their minds are not being healed from their own negative thoughts. Positivity heals in many ways. First and foremost, it's about redirecting our thoughts.

For instance, one way to focus our thoughts during meditation is to use affirmations. In religious terms, affirmations are professions. To profess something is an act of openly declaring or publicly claiming a belief.

We begin by professing a belief to ourselves first. We empty the cache of our personal computer, our subconscious mind, of evil thoughts and replacing them with good thoughts. Here is an example of a simple declaration, a profession, an affirmation.

- ✓ May you be healthy
- ✓ May you have peace of mind
- ✓ May you get that job you want

I used the word "you" here, but we would insert a person's name. May Bill have peace of mind. These affirmations sound like asking for something in a prayer, don't they? The answer is yes. Buddhism calls it meditation. Prayer and meditation are the same under different names. Both use affirmations, professions, and declarations.

Asking for others to be healthy and have peace of mind redirects us from ill will to goodwill. It is easy to ask for goodwill toward those we already like, but both Buddha and Jesus teach us that it is about asking for goodwill toward those we may not like or those who may have wronged us.

It changes our attitude toward those we may not currently see in a positive light. It removes the thoughts and emotions of anger, hate, and revenge. Those things poison our minds and bodies. Those things release damaging chemicals like cortisol and adrenaline. We are healing ourselves first.

For hatred can never put an end to hatred;
love alone can. This is an unalterable law.
~Buddha, *The Dhammapada*[2]

See how we counter hate with love? It does not require a reciprocal person-to-person agreement to hug it out. It starts internally, in our thoughts. Then, acting in alignment with those thoughts might someday lead to a mutual love and respect for one another.

Insight For Success

Meditation is not about emptying our minds, at least not in the way most people have come to understand it. Similarly, prayer is not about asking for things. We have to get this part right, or people will try to empty their minds through meditation, which is impossible. Asking for materialistic or other things through prayer is not what it is about.

Without insight, an intuitive understanding, we get confused. We align these teachings with religion, and if we have built an aversion to the concept of religion, we might avoid meditation, prayer, and affirmations. Remember, atheism is a religion.

Under misguided beliefs, what seem to be contradictions create confusion and raise the level of complexity. Then we wonder why people are so darned confused or just plain not interested. They say it's all nonsense for whack-a-doodles. Scientifically, nothing could be farther from the truth.

Until you make the unconscious conscious, it will direct your life and you will call it fate. ~Carl Jung

If you are unfamiliar with Jung, he was a Swiss psychologist and psychiatrist who founded analytical psychology. He developed the concepts of the extroverted and introverted personality archetypes and the collective unconscious. His works have had a massive influence on the study of religion and multiple fields of psychiatry. Much of Jung's work scientifically supports what Taoism, Buddhism, Greek philosophers, and the *Bible* told us thousands of years ago.

Jung's quote tells us all we need to know in the simplest terms. You can call it affirmations, meditation, or praying. It all leads to the same outcome when we understand its true purpose: acting in leadership.

You must feed your brain and exercise your brain to be in a positive state more often than a negative one, or it's like eating crappy and not exercising your body, then wondering why you're fat. Or spending more than you make, accumulating debt, and then wondering why you're financially unhealthy.

> *Your worst enemy cannot harm you as much as your own unguarded thoughts.* ~Gautama Buddha

CHAPTER THIRTY-EIGHT

Basics Of Meditation, Prayer, and Affirmations

We can immediately begin to act in leadership in three areas of our lives.

1) Our physical health – Physical activity and eating healthy foods in healthy quantities are the take-action systems for a healthier you.

2) Our financial health – Saving a little each week and not accumulating debt are the take-action systems for being financially healthy.

3) Our mental health – Affirmations, prayer, and meditation are the take-action systems for obtaining a healthy, calm, and peaceful mind.

Having common sense means you have sound judgment in practical matters. Progressing toward and maintaining a physically healthier you is sound judgment. How to eat healthily and exercise is common knowledge.

Progressing toward and maintaining a financially healthier you is sound judgment. How to save money and refrain from accumulating debt is common knowledge.

Although there is an abundance of information on a subject, this does not mean it is common knowledge. Common knowledge is when a significant number of people in society know about that subject.

I could write another health or personal finance book, but that would be unnecessary because it is common knowledge. Even though there may be abundant knowledge about our beliefs and subconscious mind, the intuitive understanding and take-action component are not common knowledge.

For you, the reader, lack of knowledge regarding your ability to impact your thoughts and subconscious minds is no longer the case. The last four chapters provided an ample amount of insight into this matter.

Due to the extensive and potentially confusing information about meditation, prayer, and affirmations floating around on the Internet, the level of complexity can quickly rise. Everyone should begin with the basics.

Prayer and meditation must include affirmations that state you are already that which you want to become. The statement must also be positive. There is science behind this approach.

Here are some simple lists that will help you get started. Use these lists or create your own. Keep your list handy and affirm your beliefs multiple times a day. Remember to keep it simple.

Thankful and Grateful

I am thankful for being alive,
I am thankful for my sight
I am thankful for my hearing
I am thankful for food
I am thankful for personal freedoms
I am thankful for pain
I am thankful for adversity & challenges
I am thankful for rain
I am thankful for sunshine
I am thankful for my job
I am thankful for my right to vote

Practice Positivity About Others

May you be healthy
May you have peace of mind
May you get that job
I like your... (outfit, hair, smile, attitude)
Great effort on...
Bob, you are a good person
Tammy, you listen well

Beliefs - Part One

I believe...
I create my life: the good and the bad
For things to change, I must change
To be a better person, I must get better

My choices create my life
My beliefs and my thoughts drive my actions
My actions determine the trajectory of my life.
Worry is a waste of time
I have control over my life
I am in control of my thoughts
My attitude is contagious
I take responsibility for my life

Beliefs - Part Two

I believe...
I am smart
I am thoughtful
I am helpful
I am patient
I am confident
I am respectful to those around me
I like my job
I like my neighbors
I love to workout
I love to eat healthy
I love the United States Constitution
I love the United States Bill of Rights
I live a healthy life
I eat healthy

Like a farmer, you plant the seeds. What you plant grows. Things are already being planted. You get to be in control. Take control.

CHAPTER THIRTY-NINE

Final Thoughts

The final nine chapters of this book provided examples that help us understand what constitutes acting in leadership. If you begin with the basics in all three of those areas, your life will change dramatically because you have begun to act in leadership.

All the components, the information for defining when a person acts in leadership, have existed for thousands of years. We misguidedly attached leadership to positions in hierarchies and doing business.

Anyone, anywhere, regardless of their age, race, ethnicity, or gender, can be a leader. Acting in leadership accomplishes this. A position in a hierarchy is not required. The BASIC™ Leadership blueprint allows us to determine when we act in leadership.

Leadership is not a static state but a dynamic process. Each of us has the potential to move in and out of acting in leadership, and therefore, in and out of being a leader at any given moment. The ultimate goal is for everyone to strive towards acting in leadership more each day.

I have provided the evidence to support my claim of what constitutes acting in leadership. You get to decide. Think for yourself. What do you believe? No matter what those beliefs might be, they will drive your actions, and through those actions, you will progress in a positive or negative trajectory. Your life will be the sum of your thoughts and your actions.

This BASIC™ Leadership blueprint defines when we are acting in leadership. Acting in leadership does not require a long, detailed plan to begin working toward worthy ideals. That may be the hardest concept to grasp because we have been fed so much misguided information about both leadership and goal setting. Then add in how we have been propagandized *not to act in leadership*, and we get the society we have today.

What you believe about the concept of leadership will determine what actions you take. Through those actions, you will gain insight. That insight, along with your actions, will determine the progression of all areas of your life. You will inevitably collaborate with someone or something during that progression. That defines life in a nutshell. Passing through the integrity hub as you move randomly from one component to another component while existing on the positive side of the leadership lifeline defines when a person is acting in leadership.

Books

Many of my readers requested a quick reference for the resources used or mentioned in my books. Here are eighteen resources listed in alphabetical order.

- ✓ *Abolishing Performance Appraisals: Why They Backfire and What To Do Instead* (2000). Tom Coens, Mary Jenkins
- ✓ *Atomic Habits: An Easy & Proven Way to Build Good Habits & Break Bad Ones* (2018). James Clear
- ✓ *The Blue Zones: Secrets for Living Longer* (2010). Dan Buettner
- ✓ *Biology of Belief: Unleashing the Power of Consciousness, Matter, & Miracles* (2005). Dr. Bruce Lipton
- ✓ *Buddha's Brain: The Practical Neuroscience of Happiness, Love, and Wisdom* (2009). Rick Hanson, PhD., and Richard Mendius, MD.
- ✓ *Captains of Consciousness: Advertising and the Social Roots of the Consumer Culture* (1976, 2001). Stuart Ewen
- ✓ *The Dhammapada* (2007). Eknath Easwaran
- ✓ *Emotional Intelligence 2.0* (2009). Jean Greaves, Travis Bradberry

✓ *Emotional Intelligence: Why It Can Matter More Then IQ* (1995, 2005). Daniel Goleman

✓ *The Four Noble Truths* (1994). Ven Lobsang Gyatso

✓ *From Stress to Strength: How to Lighten Your Load and Save Your Life* (1995). Robert S. Eliot, M.D.

✓ *The Healing Brain: Breakthrough discoveries about how the brain keeps us healthy* (1999). Robert Ornstein, David Sobel

✓ *Is it worth Dying For: How to Make Stress Work For You—Not Against You* (1984,1989). Robert S. Eliot, M.D.

✓ *Power of Habit: Why We do What We Do in Life and Business* (2012). Charles Duhigg

✓ *Propaganda* (1928). Edward Bernays

✓ *The Slight Edge: Turning Simple Disciplines into Massive Success and Happiness* (2005). Jeff Olson

✓ *Tao Te Ching: The Taoism of Lao Tzu Explained* (2011). Stefan Stenudd

✓ *What the Buddha Taught* (1974). Walpola Rahula,

References

Chapter 15: History of Acting in Leadership – Buddha

1) Buddha (1987, 2007). *The Dhammapada*. Translated by Eknath Easwaran. Tomales, CA: Nilgiri Press. Chapter 17, verse 221

Chapter 16: History of Acting in Leadership – Lao Tzu

1) Lao Tzu (2011, 2015). *Tao Te Ching*. Translated by Stefan Stenudd. Malmo, Sweden: Arriba. Chapter 68

Chapter 18: History of Acting In Leadership – Jesus & the Bible

1) Holy Bible, New International Version®, NIV®. Copyright © 1973, 1978, 1984, 2011 by Biblica, Inc.™

Chapter 21: Divergent & Manusmriti

1) Lao Tzu (2011, 2015). *Tao Te Ching*. Translated by Stefan Stenudd. Malmo, Sweden: Arriba. Chapter 32
2) Buddha (1987, 2007). *The Dhammapada*. Translated by Eknath Easwaran. Tomales, CA: Nilgiri Press. Chapter 26, verse 389
3) Lao Tzu (2011, 2015). *Tao Te Ching*. Translated by Stefan Stenudd. Malmo, Sweden: Arriba. Chapter 57

4) Buddha (1987, 2007). *The Dhammapada.* Translated by Eknath Easwaran. Tomales, CA: Nilgiri Press. Chapter 12, verses 158 - 160

Chapter 22: Time, Effort, Trade-Offs, and Guarantees

1) Lao Tzu (2015. *Tao Te Ching.* Translated by Grand Jaguar. Thornton, CO: Blackstone Publishing. Chapter 63
2) Buddha (1987, 2007). *The Dhammapada.* Translated by Eknath Easwaran. Tomales, CA: Nilgiri Press. Chapter 13, verses 168-169
3) Ross, W. D., (1925) Translation. The Internet Classic Archives. Nicomachean Ethics by Aristotle. Retrieved from http://classics.mit.edu//Aristotle/nicomachaen.html
4) Buddha (1987, 2007). *The Dhammapada.* Translated by Eknath Easwaran. Tomales, CA: Nilgiri Press. Chapter 9, verses 119-120
5) Aristotle (2015). *Rhetoric Aristotle.* Translated by W. Rhys Roberts. Fairhope, AL: Mockingbird Classic Publishing.

Chapter 23: Progression or Escalation?

1) Lao Tzu (2011, 2015). *Tao Te Ching.* Translated by Stefan Stenudd. Malmo, Sweden: Arriba. Chapter 71
2) Buddha (1987, 2007). *The Dhammapada.* Translated by Eknath Easwaran. Tomales, CA: Nilgiri Press. Chapter 24, verses 334-336

Chapter 25: Positive or Negative?

1) Buddha (1987, 2007). *The Dhammapada.* Translated by Eknath Easwaran. Tomales, CA: Nilgiri Press. Chapter 3, verse 42

2) Buddha (1987, 2007). *The Dhammapada.* Translated by Eknath Easwaran. Tomales, CA: Nilgiri Press. Chapter 22, verse 316

Chapter 26: Our Subconscious and Our Habits

1) Durant, W., (1926). *The Story of Philosophy:* New York City, NY: Pocket Books, Simon & Schuster
2) Buddha (1987, 2007). *The Dhammapada.* Translated by Eknath Easwaran. Tomales, CA: Nilgiri Press. Chapter 9, verses 117-118
3) Lao Tzu (2011, 2015). *Tao Te Ching.* Translated by Stefan Stenudd. Malmo, Sweden: Arriba. Chapter 38
4) Lao Tzu (2011, 2015). *Tao Te Ching.* Translated by Stefan Stenudd. Malmo, Sweden: Arriba. Chapter 63
5) Holy Bible, New International Version®, NIV®. Copyright © 1973, 1978, 1984, 2011 by Biblica, Inc.™

Chapter 27: Backward in Time

1) Buddha (1987, 2007). *The Dhammapada.* Translated by Eknath Easwaran. Tomales, CA: Nilgiri Press. Chapter 12, verse 165
2) Aristotle (1908). *Nicomachean Ethics.* Translated by W.D. Ross. Oxford: Clarendon Press. Book III, Part I

Chapter 28: Awareness

1) Lao Tzu (2011, 2015). *Tao Te Ching.* Translated by Stefan Stenudd. Malmo, Sweden: Arriba. Chapter 33
2) Buddha (1987, 2007). *The Dhammapada.* Translated by Eknath Easwaran. Tomales, CA: Nilgiri Press. Chapter 12, verses 158-159
3) *The Bible.* New International Version, Biblica, Inc., 1978,1984, 2011.

Chapter 29: Practical Application

1) Buddha (1987, 2007). *The Dhammapada.* Translated by Eknath Easwaran. Tomales, CA: Nilgiri Press. Chapter 15, verse 204
2) Lao Tzu (2011, 2015). *Tao Te Ching.* Translated by Stefan Stenudd. Malmo, Sweden: Arriba. Chapter 13
3) Holy Bible, New International Version®, NIV®. Copyright © 1973, 1978, 1984, 2011 by Biblica, Inc.™
4) Hippocrates (1931). *Regimine.* Translated by W.H.S. Jones. London: William Heinemann; New York : G.P. Putnam's Sons

Chapter 32: Goal Setting For Life

1) Holy Bible, New International Version®, NIV®. Copyright © 1973, 1978, 1984, 2011 by Biblica, Inc.™
2) Lao Tzu (2011, 2015). *Tao Te Ching.* Translated by Stefan Stenudd. Malmo, Sweden: Arriba. Chapter 63
3) Buddha (1987, 2007). *The Dhammapada.* Translated by Eknath Easwaran. Tomales, CA: Nilgiri Press. Chapter 12, verse 165
4) Buddha (1987, 2007). *The Dhammapada.* Translated by Eknath Easwaran. Tomales, CA: Nilgiri Press. Chapter 20, verse 280
5) Buddha (1987, 2007). *The Dhammapada.* Translated by Eknath Easwaran. Tomales, CA: Nilgiri Press. Chapter 21, verse 292
6) Hesiod (1914). *Works and Days.* Translated by Hugh G. Evelyn-White.

Chapter 33: BASIC Finances – Acting In Leadership

1) Aesop (1916). *Aesop's Fables.* Translated by V. S. Vernon Jones. London: London William Heinemann; New York: Double Day Page & Co.
2) Buddha (1987, 2007). *The Dhammapada.* Translated by Eknath Easwaran. Tomales, CA: Nilgiri Press. Chapter 20, verses 274-276
3) Holy Bible, New International Version®, NIV®. Copyright © 1973, 1978, 1984, 2011 by Biblica, Inc.™
4) Lao Tzu (2011, 2015). *Tao Te Ching.* Translated by Stefan Stenudd. Malmo, Sweden: Arriba. Chapter 46
5) Buddha (1987, 2007). *The Dhammapada.* Translated by Eknath Easwaran. Tomales, CA: Nilgiri Press. Chapter 16, verses 211-212
6) Aesop (1916). *Aesop's Fables.* Translated by V. S. Vernon Jones. London: London William Heinemann; New York: Double Day Page & Co.

Chapter 34: Power of the Mind – Part One

1) Stobaeus (1916-1918). *The Greek Anthology.* Translated by W. R. Patton. London: W. Heinemann; New York, G.P. Putnam's Sons
2) Holy Bible, New International Version®, NIV®. Copyright © 1973, 1978, 1984, 2011 by Biblica, Inc.™
3) Buddha (1987, 2007). *The Dhammapada.* Translated by Eknath Easwaran. Tomales, CA: Nilgiri Press. Chapter 12, verse 165
4) Lao Tzu (2011, 2015). *Tao Te Ching.* Translated by Stefan Stenudd. Malmo, Sweden: Arriba. Chapter 71

Chapter 36: Meditation, Prayer, and Affirmations

1) Buddha (1987, 2007). *The Dhammapada.* Translated by Eknath Easwaran. Tomales, CA: Nilgiri Press. Chapter 2, verses 24-27
2) Aristotle (1908). *Nicomachean Ethics.* Translated by W.D. Ross. Oxford: Clarendon Press. Book V, Part I
3) Lao Tzu (2011, 2015). *Tao Te Ching.* Translated by Stefan Stenudd. Malmo, Sweden: Arriba. Chapter 16

Chapter 37: Misconceptions about Meditation, Prayer, and Affirmations

1) Holy Bible, New International Version®, NIV®. Copyright © 1973, 1978, 1984, 2011 by Biblica, Inc.™
2) Buddha (1987, 2007). *The Dhammapada.* Translated by Eknath Easwaran. Tomales, CA: Nilgiri Press. Chapter 1, verse 5